Meriwether Lewis

William Clark

THE WORLD'S GREAT EXPLORERS

Meriwether Lewis and William Clark

By Christine A. Fitz-Gerald

CHILDRENS PRESS ®

CHICAGO

*Early Indian petroglyphs, or rock
pictures, near Lewiston, Idaho, a
site where Lewis and Clark camped
in 1805*

Project Editor: Ann Heinrichs
Designer: Lindaanne Donohoe
Cover Art: Steven Gaston Dobson
Engraver: Liberty Photoengraving

**Library of Congress
Cataloging-in-Publication Data**

Fitz-Gerald, Christine Maloney.
    Meriwether Lewis and William Clark / by
Christine A. Fitz-Gerald.
        p. cm — (The World's great explorers)
    Includes bibliographical references and index.
    Summary: Describes the expedition made by
Lewis and Clark in which they journeyed from
Saint Louis to the Pacific.
    ISBN 0-516-03061-2
    1. Explorers—West (U.S.)—Biography—Juve-
nile literature. 2. Lewis, Meriwether, 1774-1809—
Juvenile literature. 3. Clark, William, 1770-
1838—Juvenile literature. 4. Lewis and Clark
Expedition (1804-1806)—Juvenile literature. 5.
West (U.S.)—Description and travel—To 1848—
Juvenile literature. 6. United States—Exploring
expeditions—Juvenile literature. [1. Lewis,
Meriwether, 1774-1809. 2. Clark, William, 1770-
1838. 3. Lewis and Clark Expedition (1804-1806).
4. Explorers.] I. Title. II. Series.
F592.7.F57 1991
910'.92'2—dc20   90-20696
[B]   CIP
[92]   AC

Lewis and Clark among the Mandans

Table of Contents

Chapter 1 "Ocean in View!". 6

Chapter 2 Beginnings. 14

Chapter 3 Plans and Preparations. 22

Chapter 4 The Big Muddy. 34

Chapter 5 Fort Mandan. 46

Chapter 6 The High Plains. 54

Chapter 7 Across the Rockies and Beyond. 72

Chapter 8 Homeward Bound. 86

Chapter 9 Journey's End. 94

Chapter 10 Different Paths. .108

Appendix. 120

Timeline of Events in Lewis's and Clark's Lifetimes. . . .122

Glossary of Terms. 123

Bibliography. 124

Index. 125

Chapter 1
"Ocean in View!"

Four dugouts rode the strong current of the Columbia River westward. A small, swift canoe ran ahead of the clumsy dugouts to scout the river. Rain fell on the explorers— thirty-three people and a dog—as the Lewis and Clark expedition headed through the lush rain forest of the Pacific Northwest coastal region.

They were in a no-man's-land, an area claimed by several countries, the United States among them. The land stretching north of the Columbia would one day be part of Washington State; the land to the south would be in Oregon.

November 7, 1805, was chilly and gray. The day had begun in a dense fog that lifted slowly. It was afternoon before the men could clearly see the land through which they were traveling. Steep hills edged the riverbank; there was not enough level land to provide a comfortable campsite. A forest of massive trees—firs, cedars, and hemlock—stretched into the distance. The forest floor was carpeted with vines, ferns, and underbrush.

Thomas Jefferson

The Pacific Northwest rain forest thrived on the persistent rainfall that made the Lewis and Clark expedition so uncomfortable. For almost two weeks, they had traveled in wet clothes and slept in wet blankets. Rain seeped into their food and supplies. Despite everything, the mood of the explorers was cheerful because they knew that the Pacific Ocean was near.

The Pacific Ocean had been their destination when they began their journey from Camp Wood, Missouri. The men had built Camp Wood themselves on the bank of the Mississippi River, opposite the mouth of the Missouri River, not far north of the city of St. Louis. On May 14, 1804, they left Camp Wood in three boats. A small crowd waved and shouted to them from the shore. The men of the Lewis and Clark expedition fired a small cannon in salute, rowed across the Mississippi, and nosed their boats into the Missouri, pulling hard against the oncoming current. Now eighteen months had passed in a difficult, dangerous journey across the North American continent. The Scottish explorer Alexander Mackenzie had crossed Canada to the Pacific in 1792–1793. Now Lewis and Clark hoped to be the first to reach the ocean traveling through United States territory.

Captains Meriwether Lewis and William Clark, the leaders of the expedition, were professional soldiers. Both born in Virginia, they met while serving at the small frontier outpost of Fort Greenville, Ohio, in the 1790s. There they became friends despite their many differences. In 1801, Meriwether Lewis became President Thomas Jefferson's personal secretary. When Jefferson asked Lewis to head an expedition of discovery across the wild, unmapped lands west of the

Mississippi, Lewis accepted eagerly. Since the trip would be dangerous, Lewis thought it would be wise to have two leaders. Lewis believed his friend William Clark would make a good co-captain and partner. Clark agreed to join the expedition, and the remarkable partnership of Lewis and Clark began.

The success of the expedition would depend largely on how well its leaders worked together. Lewis and Clark shared their leadership without jealousy or rivalry. They reached decisions together smoothly. In fact, they never disagreed on anything of importance. Both men were very bright, although their talents lay in different areas.

Meriwether Lewis had more formal education than did Clark. In his five years of formal schooling, he had learned mathematics, geography, and some astronomy. He was an outstanding amateur naturalist. Since boyhood, he had been a curious observer of plant and animal life.

Later throughout the expedition, Meriwether Lewis wrote accurate descriptions of new plants and animals that he found. When it was possible, he sent specimens of plant and animal life back to President Jefferson, who was also an avid naturalist. Lewis was tall—over 6 feet (1.8 meters)—slender, and dark-haired. He did not have an easy personality but was moody and impatient.

William Clark, on the other hand, was sociable and even-tempered. Although he was not as well educated as Lewis, he brought a wealth of practical skills and shrewd intelligence to the expedition. He was an expert riverboatman, and he was good at dealing with the Indians, perhaps because he liked them. Clark also proved to be a genius at geography.

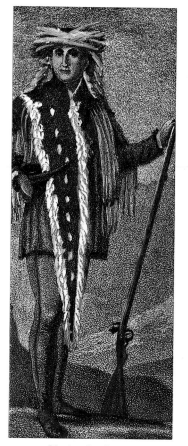

Meriwether Lewis

The explorers had no accurate maps to show them the way. Instead, they had to rely on Indian legends, trappers' stories, and their own instincts. Clark was not only good at finding the right way to take, but he also drew remarkably accurate maps of the country through which they passed. Like Lewis, Clark was over six feet tall, but he was stockier in build and had bright red hair. At the time they left Camp Wood, Lewis was twenty-nine years old and Clark was thirty-three.

Almost all of those in the dugouts were young soldiers who had volunteered for the expedition. The captains wanted young, unmarried men for this dangerous journey. In addition to the two captains and twenty-six soldiers, there were five others: a young Indian woman named Sacajawea; her infant son, Jean Baptiste, whom everyone called Pomp; her husband, the Frenchman Touissant Charbonneau; William Clark's black slave York; and another Frenchman hired as a hunter and interpreter. Lewis also brought his black Newfoundland dog, Seaman.

Twice earlier that chilly November day, they had stopped at Indian villages to buy food and animal skins. At the first village, they were able to buy fish, edible roots called wapatoo, three dogs, and some otter skins. Eating dog meat was one of the few things about which Lewis and Clark could not agree. Lewis found it to be delicious, similar in taste to beaver, but Clark never got used to it.

The local Indian tribes—Chinook, Sokulk, Clatsop, and Tillamook—depended on fish for their living. Each year, from April to October, the salmon migrated upriver to their spawning grounds to lay their eggs. During the salmon run, the Indians caught enough

York, Clark's slave

fish to last a year. Some they dried, and some they pounded into a powder. By the time Lewis and Clark reached the Pacific Northwest, the salmon run was over. A constant diet of fish powder and roots became monotonous. Most of the men were happy at the chance to eat dog meat.

"York," a painting by Montana artist Charles M. Russell

Clark was pleased that in the second Indian village he was able to buy "2 beaver skins for the purpose of making me a robe as the robe I have is rotten and good for nothing." It troubled the captains that their supply of goods to trade with the Indians had run so low. They had brought thimbles, bells, mirrors, fishhooks, hatchets, kettles, and scarlet cloth, but they wished they had brought more. Most of the beads they had left were red or white. They had very few of the blue beads that the Indians prized as "chief beads."

If they had had more trade goods, they would have given them happily for canoes. Their own dugouts were awkward, slow, and hard to maneuver. The men had made the dugouts themselves, hollowing each from a single large tree. Bobbing along in their crude craft, they admired the swift Indian canoes. The canoes could carry many people and large loads, not only in the rivers but also in the high waves of the Pacific. The Indians asked such high prices for their canoes that Lewis and Clark had been able to purchase only one very small one.

Lewis and Clark were in a hurry to reach the ocean. They hoped that a British or American trading ship would be anchored offshore. Then they could ask for food and supplies or even for a ride home by sea. The explorers had seen many signs that the ocean was near. They had seen sea otters, which inhabited Pacific coastal areas. They had also seen Indians wearing sailor jackets, indicating trade with European people, and Indians whose noses were pierced with seashells. The Columbia River rose and fell with the tide, and its water was too salty to drink.

Rounding a bend in the Columbia, the men saw a splendid sight. Just ahead, the river poured into a huge body of water. The water stretched out in the distance for as far as the eye could see. High waves beat on the shore. Elated, William Clark jotted in his notebook, "Ocean in view! O! the joy."

Believing this was the Pacific, the men camped for the night. Clark wrote: "Great joy in camp. We are in view of the Ocean, this great Pacific Ocean which we have been so long anxious to see, and the roaring or noise made by the waves breaking on the rocky shores (as I suppose) may be heard distinctly."

In fact, the explorers had only reached Gray's Bay, where the Columbia River widens out in its final rush to the ocean. The Pacific itself was still 20 miles (32 kilometers) distant. Rough weather and high waves kept the explorers from reaching it for over a week. Then not all of the men cared to go.

Lewis and Clark, however, would not have missed seeing the ocean for anything. Lewis reached it first, on November 14 or 15, 1805. Impatient as always, he went ahead by canoe and then by foot when the waves threatened to capsize his canoe. When Lewis returned, Clark set out with eleven men on November 18. They walked twenty miles to gaze upon the ocean. Clark wrote that the "men appear much satisfied with their trip, beholding with astonishment the high waves dashing against the rocks and this immense ocean." The continent had been crossed!

The Pacific Ocean washing the northern Oregon coast

Chapter 2
Beginnings

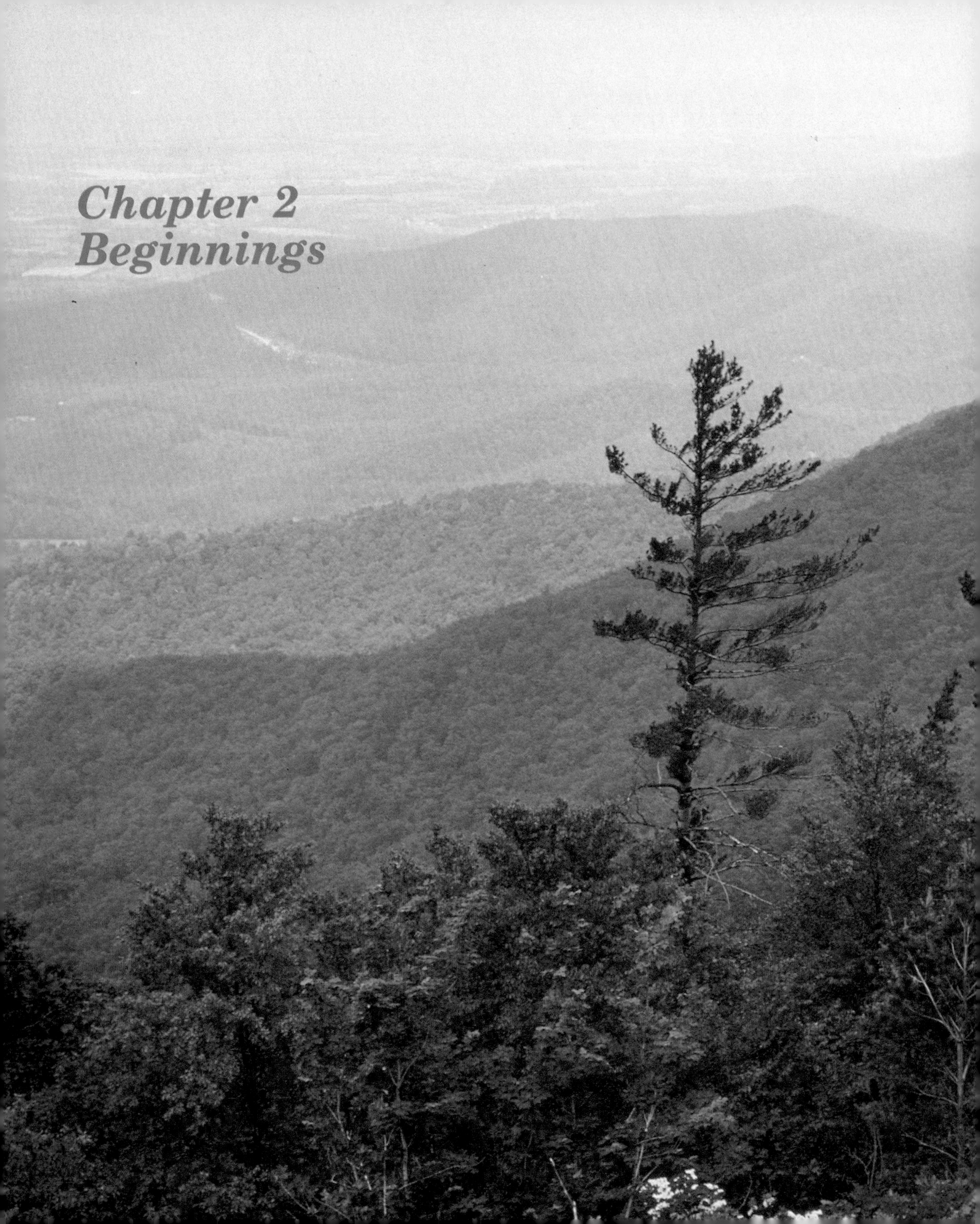

Albemarle County, Virginia, had a mild climate, rich soil, and abundant water. It was a farmer's paradise. Not all of the county was neat fields and orchards; the foothills of the Blue Ridge Mountains were home to wolves, elk, deer, and Indians.

Meriwether Lewis was born in the family home, Locust Hill, on August 18, 1774. He was the second of Lucy and John Lewis's three children. The Lewises had a famous neighbor, Thomas Jefferson, who lived at his nearby home, Monticello.

Before Meriwether was one year old, war broke out between the American colonies and Great Britain. His father enlisted to fight against the British in the American War of Independence. Returning home on leave in November 1779, Lieutenant Lewis reached a flooded river. In his great hurry to see his family, he swam his horse across it. Thoroughly wet and chilled, John Lewis became ill and died of pneumonia within two days. Meriwether Lewis was five years old when his father died.

Lucy Lewis, left alone with three young children and a plantation to run, quickly remarried. Her new husband, Captain John Marks, moved the family to Georgia after the war. Georgia was much less densely settled than Virginia had been. Meriwether hunted, fished, and roamed the woods, sometimes going out alone at night with his dogs and his gun. He became familiar with all the plants and animals in the area. His interests were encouraged by his mother, who was an "herb doctor." She grew and gathered herbs that she used to treat illnesses, and her homemade medicines were in great demand.

Meriwether Lewis needed to know more than wilderness lore, but Georgia had no schools at the time. In 1787, at the age of thirteen, he returned alone to Virginia to attend school and to learn to manage the family plantation, which his father had left to him. For the next five years, Lewis attended schools taught by local ministers. Peachy Gilmer, a classmate, described him: "He was always remarkable for perseverance which in the early period of his life seemed nothing more than obstinacy in pursuing the trifles that employ that age: a martial temper; a great steadfastness of purpose, self possession, and undaunted courage. His person was stiff and without grace, bow legged, awkward, formal and almost without flexibility; his face was comely and considered by many handsome."

By age eighteen, Lewis had left school and was a gentleman farmer and the head of a large household. His stepfather had died, and Lewis had brought his mother back to Locust Hill, along with his sister Jane, his brother Reuben, his half-brother John Hastings Marks, and his half-sister Mary Marks.

A Virginia plantation was more than a farm. It was likely to have its own carpentry shop, blacksmith shop, and corn mill. Plantations produced their own soap, cloth, and food. Locust Hill was a scene of ceaseless activity. Wool was spun into thread and the thread woven into cloth. Hogs were butchered and made into sausage and ham. The gardens—herb, flower, and vegetable—were tended constantly. The main house, barns, stables, tool sheds, and tobacco-drying sheds needed to be kept in good repair. Lewis managed Locust Hill well, but the routine of plantation life made him restless.

A Virginia homestead

George Washington

In 1794, President George Washington asked for volunteers to help suppress rioting in Pennsylvania, where farmers were protesting a hefty new tax on whiskey. Lewis joined the Virginia militia immediately. The Whiskey Rebellion, as it became known, was put down with no loss of life. Lewis enjoyed this taste of military life, so he transferred to the regular army. Ensign Lewis was assigned to a rifle company in Fort Greenville, Ohio. The commanding officer was Captain William Clark. Shortly afterwards, Clark retired from military life, but not before he and Meriwether Lewis had become fast friends.

Lewis was never in combat, but he supervised the construction of a fort near present-day Memphis, Tennessee. This experience would prove useful to him later. He also gained experience in military drilling, which bored the men but prepared them to respond well in an emergency. He advanced rapidly and, by the age of twenty-six, was a captain stationed in Detroit, Michigan.

In 1801, Thomas Jefferson became the third president of the United States. As president, he had to choose men to fill a number of government jobs. Jefferson was impressed with his neighbor Meriwether Lewis. Lewis had been a successful farmer and had done well in the army, too. He shared Jefferson's interests in science and natural history. Politically, he was, like Jefferson, a Republican. Most importantly, Lewis was a man of good character, someone who could be trusted. Jefferson invited Lewis to become his personal secretary, saying, "Your knowledge of the Western Country, of the army and of all its interests and relations have rendered it desirable for public as well as private purposes that you should be engaged in that office." Delighted to accept, Lewis was in Washington by early April, 1801.

The Clarks had lived in Albemarle County, Virginia, for some time, but they moved to a larger farm on the Rappahannock River before William Clark was born. John and Ann Clark had a large family. William, born on August 1, 1770, was the ninth of ten children. His five older brothers fought in the American Revolutionary War. William was much too young to fight. One of his brothers, George Rogers Clark, achieved fame as a revolutionary war general.

The Clarks were among the many families that migrated west over the Appalachian Mountains after the war. They built a large, two-story home near Louisville, Kentucky, in 1784. Mulberry Hill, as the Clarks called their new home, was surrounded by wilderness. There, fourteen-year-old William became an expert hunter and woodsman.

Not much is known about William Clark's education. If he did not attend school before his family moved from Virginia, he certainly had no chance to attend schools in Kentucky, for there were none. Perhaps his older brothers taught him the basics of reading, writing, and arithmetic.

It was only natural for William Clark to become a soldier. Not only had all of his brothers been soldiers, but Kentucky was a dangerous place in the 1780s. The Indians were angry at being pushed from their tribal lands. Settlers lived in constant fear of attack. Many families were killed in sudden, swift Indian raids. The regular U.S. Army was too small to protect the entire frontier. That job fell to the local militia, which Clark joined at age nineteen. He fought in several skirmishes with the Indians.

George Rogers Clark

"Mad" Anthony Wayne

Eventually, President Washington decided to bring local militias into the regular army. Clark then became a lieutenant in the army of General "Mad" Anthony Wayne. Wayne was anything but mad when it came to fighting Indians. He was careful, alert, and patient. Clark learned a great deal from Wayne about traveling safely in Indian country. Wayne sent Clark down the Mississippi River in a canoe to spy on the Spaniards, who were thought to be building a fort near modern-day Memphis, Tennessee. Later he commanded a rifle company at Fort Greenville, Ohio, where he met Meriwether Lewis.

The Indian wars in that area ended in 1794 with Wayne's victory at the Battle of Fallen Timbers. The excitement of army life soon faded for Clark. Peacetime army life seemed to be all drills, inspections, and boredom. Also, his older brother George Rogers Clark needed help in straightening out his personal finances. So William Clark left the army on July 1, 1796. Army life had taught him much. He had drawn maps, built forts, commanded men. He had become an excellent boatman and rifle shot. He knew the value of caution when traveling in hostile territory, and he had fought Indians without hating them, as some settlers did.

Clark settled into a routine life in Clarksville, Indiana, just across the Ohio River from Louisville. When his father died in 1799, William took over the family farm. He inherited 9,000 acres (3,642 hectares) and some slaves, one of whom was named York.

William Clark and Meriwether Lewis exchanged letters from time to time. Family business occasionally took Clark to Washington, where he visited Lewis, the president's secretary. Clark met President Jefferson on one of these trips.

On one trip, Clark met two young girls—cousins—on a back country road in Virginia. Julia Hancock and Harriet Kennerly were having no luck riding a stubborn horse until Clark stopped to help them. After this one short meeting, Clark could not forget twelve-year-old Julia. He misheard her name as Judy, later naming the Judith River after her.

A letter from Lewis in June 1803 changed Clark's life. Lewis wrote of an exciting trip that he had been appointed to lead. Clark felt a twinge of envy because he loved an adventure, too. Not until the end of the letter did Lewis ask Clark to join him as an equal leader: "If therefore, there is anything . . . which would induce you to participate with me in its fatigues, its dangers and its honors, believe me there is no man on earth with whom I should feel equal pleasure in sharing them as with yourself." Clark fired back an enthusiastic letter: "My friend, I join you with hand and heart."

Clark's letter of acceptance to Meriwether Lewis

Chapter 3
Plans and Preparations

Embarking on the western expedition would mean an absence of two to three years, and Meriwether Lewis had not given William Clark long to prepare. He made his offer of joint leadership in late June 1803 and planned to pick Clark up by keelboat in late August. If Clark felt that things were happening fast, Lewis felt that everything was taking too long. He and President Jefferson had been planning the journey in secret since late 1801 or early 1802. Jefferson set the overall objectives, but Lewis was in charge of the practical business of getting outfitted. It was quite a challenge. Neither he nor anyone else knew exactly what sort of country lay ahead of them. The party had to take the right supplies and in the right quantities—as much as they needed but no more than they could easily transport.

In February 1803, Congress set aside $2,500 for the expedition. Lewis enlisted the help of government purchasing agents to buy supplies. He bought most of what he needed in Philadelphia but got weapons from the government arsenal in Harpers Ferry, Virginia (now West Virginia). The explorers would need good guns, both to hunt game and to protect themselves. Because he was not satisfied with the guns that were available, Lewis designed a rifle that was exactly what he had in mind. The custom-made rifle was so good that the army adopted Lewis's design. In addition to rifles and ammunition, Lewis purchased knives, cannon for the boats, and an air gun that required no powder to fire.

Lewis did not spend much money on food. According to his plan, the men would live off the land. However, he did buy some "portable soup" and barrels of salt, pork, and flour. For clothing, he purchased blankets, coats, shirts, and socks. The explorers would need camping equipment of all kinds, and Lewis included rope, nails, spades, needles, vises, and rasps. He took medicine, scientific instruments, and books.

The most costly category was gifts for the Indians. Lewis bought a staggering array of items: calico shirts, mirrors, eyeglasses, copper wire, ribbons, thimbles, brass buttons, fishhooks, jewelry, and kettles. He had soon spent $2,100 of his allotted $2,500. He had roughly 2,700 pounds (1,225 kilograms) of supplies gathered in Philadelphia and another 800 pounds (363 kilograms) waiting in Harpers Ferry. All of it had to be taken by wagon to Pittsburgh, where a boat was being built. Lewis set aside the remaining $400 to hire interpreters and guides.

Lewis felt that he needed to know more about

Model of the keelboat used by Lewis and Clark, displayed in Lewis and Clark State Park, Iowa

science for the trip, so he studied with famous naturalists and doctors. He visited Lancaster, Pennsylvania, to study celestial navigation—a method of steering a course by the stars—with an astronomer.

Everything took more time than Lewis had planned. He was furious when he arrived in Pittsburgh on July 15 and discovered that his keelboat, which was to have been finished on July 20, was hardly begun. This craft, designed by Lewis, was flat-bottomed, about 55 feet (17 meters) long, and just slightly over 4 feet (1.2 meters) wide. Lewis's keelboat would have a cabin, at least one mast, and a covered hold for baggage. There was little chance of finding a suitable keelboat farther downriver, so he had to wait for it to be finished.

Scene on the Ohio River

The summer was dry. Each day he waited, the river fell lower and lower. He was determined that a low river would not stop him. He wrote, "It shall not prevent my proceeding, being determined to get forward though I should not be able to make a greater distance than a mile a day . . . should I not be able to make greater speed than a boat's length per day."

While waiting in Pittsburgh, Lewis wrote to President Jefferson, who was anxious to hear of Lewis's progress. Jefferson had lofty expectations of the explorers. He wanted Lewis and Clark to discover a good river route across the continent.

The explorers planned to take their boats down the Ohio River until they reached the Mississippi. There they would veer north, pushing up the Mississippi to the mouth of the Missouri River. They would

follow the Missouri westward until they reached its source. Then they would portage, or carry their boats and supplies, to another river, as yet undiscovered, to continue the journey. Sea captains who had anchored off the Pacific Northwest coast told of a broad river that spilled into the sea. Jefferson hoped that this great river, or one of its tributaries, would pick up not far from where the Missouri River ended. He thought the portage from one river to the next would be short— perhaps a half-day's march.

Jefferson was not alone in hoping for a water route across the continent. It was a common belief that such a route did exist. If it were found, it would make trade with China and other Far Eastern lands much easier. As it was, trading ships spent two to three years sailing around South America to China and back.

Punch Bowl Falls pours into Eagle Creek in the Columbia River Gorge. The Columbia River was the route to the Pacific that Lewis and Clark hoped to find.

27

Lewis and Clark were to draw maps of the land and record scientific information on climate, soil, and plant and animal life. They were to establish friendly relations with all of the Indian peoples they met. Jefferson wanted to know everything possible about these Western Indians: their language, houses, appearance, religion, and customs.

Jefferson and Lewis had kept their plans secret because the expedition would cross Spanish territory. Spain owned all the land stretching from the Gulf of Mexico in the south to Canada in the north, and from the Mississippi River in the east to the Rocky Mountains in the west. This vast chunk of land was known as the Louisiana Territory. Jefferson wanted to limit the size of the party to about a dozen men and to send them off without much fanfare to avoid alarming the Spaniards, who would regard the explorers as trespassers.

The situation changed rapidly. Napoleon Bonaparte, First Consul of France, had forced Spain to give him all of this land in a secret treaty. When the terms of the treaty became known, Americans were alarmed. Spaniards had always allowed Americans to ship their goods down the Mississippi, through the port of New Orleans. The French, it appeared, would not allow the Americans this "right of deposit."

Jefferson immediately sent James Monroe off to Paris to arrange for the purchase of New Orleans and part of Florida from the French. Monroe had been authorized to spend up to ten million dollars for this relatively small piece of land. Napoleon, needing cash for his war against Great Britain, abruptly offered to sell the entire Louisiana Territory to the United States for only fifteen million dollars!

Napoleon Bonaparte

49° Boundary fixed by Ashburton Treaty, 1842.

42°

Boundary fixed by Treaty with Spain, 1819.

36° 30'

32° 30'

FROM FRANCE 1803

BY TREATY OF 1783

FROM SPAIN 1819

The United States made a great bargain in purchasing the Louisiana Territory in 1803. The purchase gave Americans another 800,000 square miles (2,072,000 square kilometers) of land, effectively doubling the size of the United States.

The land was formally transferred to the United States on March 10, 1804. Now Lewis and Clark would be exploring not Spanish but American soil, right up to the foothills of the Rocky Mountains. As a result, they could take a larger group of men with them. There was safety in numbers. Beyond the Rockies was a disputed territory, claimed by several countries. Jefferson hoped to strengthen the American claim to the area through Lewis's and Clark's exploration.

Map showing the lands received from France in the Louisiana Purchase

Lewis finally left Pittsburgh on August 31, 1803, in his keelboat, accompanied by a similar, smaller boat called a pirogue. He had managed to sign on only three volunteers at this point, so he brought along some soldiers to man the boats. Lewis hoped that Clark had found some good men. He wrote to Clark: "When descending the Ohio it shall be my duty by enquiry to find out and engage some good hunters, stout, healthy, unmarried men accustomed to the woods and capable of bearing bodily fatigue in a pretty considerable degree. Should any young men answering this description be found in your neighbourhood, I would thank you to give me information on them on my arrival at the falls of the Ohio."

The trip down the Ohio gave them a taste of the hard travel to come. The river was so low that the boats stuck on sandbars. The men frequently had to jump overboard and stand in the shallow water, pushing and pulling the boats off the bars. At times, they hired teams of oxen to tow the boats. But there were some pleasant times, too. Seaman, Lewis's dog, caught a number of squirrels as they were swimming across the river. The crew had fried squirrel for dinner and it was delicious. Lewis stopped in Wheeling, Virginia, to buy a second pirogue.

By mid-October, the party reached Clarksville, where William Clark waited with some volunteers. In Kaskaskia, Illinois, farther downriver, they selected more men from an army garrison. By the time they reached the Mississippi, there was no chance of leaving until spring, when the ice on the Missouri River would be breaking up. In December, the men built Camp Wood, 20 miles (32 kilometers) north of St. Louis, across from the mouth of the Missouri.

Anxious as they were to start, wintering at Camp Wood served a good purpose. There were forty-five or fifty men in all. Some had been soldiers before, but many were civilians. At Camp Wood, they got to know each other and learned to follow orders.

All winter the men drilled. There was constant rifle practice. Most of the training fell to Clark; Lewis was busy in St. Louis buying more supplies and talking to traders who had traveled the Missouri. Lewis even circulated a questionnaire among the trappers and traders, trying to get every scrap of information he could about the land upriver. Clark had his hands full trying to keep order among the men. Bored and at loose ends, some of them drank too much, fought among themselves, and refused to follow orders. As the winter wore on, it became clear to the captains which of the men they wanted to take on the trip.

They picked men with valuable skills. George Drouillard joined the party as a hunter, interpreter, and scout. Half French and half Shawnee, Drouillard was fluent in Indian sign language. He was the best hunter, sharpshooter, and woodsman in the entire group. John Colter was another seasoned woodsman.

Patrick Gass was a good carpenter. The Fields brothers, Reuben and Joseph, were hunters and woodsmen. William Warner could cook, and Silas Goodrich was a master fisherman. Two of the men, George Gibson and Pierre Cruzatte, played the fiddle. Their music could entertain the soldiers.

The youngest man, George Shannon, was eighteen years old. John Shields was the oldest, at age thirty-five. Shields was married and had children, but the captains included him anyway because he was a blacksmith and a gunsmith.

On May 13, Clark received disappointing news. Lewis had promised him a captain's rank and pay when he asked him to join the expedition. Army officials, though agreeing to give Clark a captain's pay, refused to promote him to captain. He and Lewis were disappointed and angry, though not with each other. They agreed to tell the men that Clark was a captain. Lewis, to his credit, always treated Clark as an equal, despite his lesser official rank.

Spring drew closer, and the tempo of activity at camp grew feverish. Gear was checked and rechecked. Supplies were packed and many things added at the last minute. Lewis and Clark made their final selections for the permanent party. They chose three sergeants—John Ordway, Nathaniel Pryor, and Charles Floyd—and twenty-two privates, who were divided into three squads.

Bear's Tooth Mountain on the Missouri River

Six soldiers under Corporal Richard Warfington would escort them some distance upriver. Nine French boatmen led by Baptiste Deschamps would go along as far as the Mandan Villages in present-day North Dakota. When the Frenchmen arrived on May 11, everyone knew that departure was imminent.

The day of departure arrived—a rainy Monday, May 14, 1804. Lewis was still in St. Louis, but he had told Clark to start without him. Lewis would ride upriver and meet them at St. Charles, Missouri. The permanent exploring party was in the large keelboat, the French rivermen manned the seven-oared red pirogue, and the soldiers under Warfington rowed the six-oared white pirogue. The men were not used to handling the heavily packed boats. They traveled only 4 miles (6.4 kilometers) before camping for the night. Nevertheless, the journey had begun.

Map of the Lewis and Clark expedition

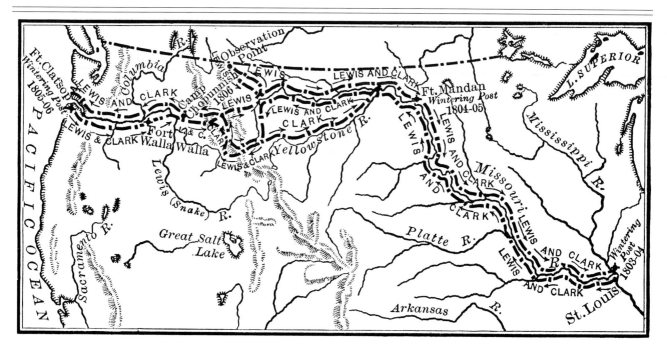

Chapter 4
The Big Muddy

The Missouri was a powerful river, fast-flowing and dangerous. It was the longest river in North America. Its rushing waters carried so much soil that they were colored a rich brown. Americans called the river "The Big Muddy." The murky waters hid many hazards; there were submerged logs and trees that could rip out the bottom of a boat.

Luckily, two experienced voyageurs, or French boatmen, had enlisted at St. Charles. Pierre Cruzatte and Francois Labiche had traveled the Missouri as far as the Platte River, some 400 to 500 miles (644 to 805 kilometers) away. The captains were delighted to have them in the party. Even so, progress was slow until all the men got used to handling the boats. At times, the current was so strong that the only way to go forward was for the men to walk along the riverbank, towing the boats with long ropes.

At first they went almost directly west through the present-day state of Missouri. Summer brought steamy hot days and violent thunderstorms. Some of the men suffered sunstroke. All were pestered by ticks and swarms of mosquitoes. From Missouri, the river looped north through modern-day Iowa.

A daily routine emerged. They averaged 15 miles (24 kilometers) a day. Clark, the better riverman, stayed aboard the keelboat, noting their course and drawing maps. Lewis, the better naturalist, was usually ashore, walking or riding one of their two horses. He studied the land through which they passed—its soil, rock formations, plants, and animals.

George Drouillard and John Shields hunted constantly to keep the men well fed. The men dined on turkeys, geese, beaver, deer, and waterfowl and on wild berries that grew on bushes by the water's edge. The three sergeants had been ordered to keep journals of the trip, and several privates decided to do the same. At night, there was time for writing around the campfire. On some nights, Pierre Cruzatte played his fiddle and the men danced.

The captains never forgot that they were in Indian country, and guards were posted every night. By the end of July, they had reached present-day Nebraska, but had not seen a single Indian. Lewis and Clark were concerned, because one of their objectives was to meet the Indians. One day, George Drouillard returned to camp with an Indian who told the captains of a nearby Oto village. La Liberte, one of the hired Frenchmen, was sent to invite the Otos to a council.

On August 2, 1804, fourteen Otos appeared, but without La Liberte, who had deserted. Men were sent after him, but he was never found. Lewis gave the

Lewis and Clark holding a council with the Indians, as drawn by Patrick Gass, a member of the expedition

Otos some roasted pork and meal, and the Otos gave the Americans some watermelons. The next day, Lewis and Clark held the first of many Indian councils under the shade of the keelboat sail, which was set up as an awning. The soldiers had dressed in full uniform to impress the Indians. Lewis told the Indians that the river and land now belonged to the Great Father in Washington. He invited the Indians to deal with the American traders who would soon appear in the wake of the expedition. Finally, he urged that the tribes make peace among themselves. The Americans gave the Otos gifts of medals, clothing, and gunpowder. A demonstration of the air gun was a great success.

Both Lewis and Clark were pleased by the council. The Indians seemed friendly and interested in trade with the Americans. Sergeant Ordway wrote in his journal that "They [the Otos] all appeared to be glad that they got freed from other powers."

Happy as they were with their meeting, both captains realized that the Otos were a friendly tribe. Each day brought them closer to the hostile and powerful Sioux. Jefferson had mentioned the Sioux specifically in a written instruction to Lewis: "On that nation we wish most particularly to make a friendly impression because of their immense power."

The Sioux controlled the James River, a major river highway for fur traders. The James was part of the great canoe trail that led all the way to British Montreal in Canada. In return for furs, the Sioux

Steering through rapids

received tools, weapons, cloth, tobacco, blankets, and whiskey. Friendly with the British, the Sioux would be hostile to American traders who might sell goods directly to other tribes. Those tribes would no longer need the Sioux as middlemen.

All was not well with the expedition as they neared the James River and the Sioux nation. Moses Reed deserted. Unlike La Liberte, he was caught and forced to run the gauntlet, passing between two lines of men who whipped him with switches. The captains expelled him from the permanent party and put him to work rowing aboard one of the pirogues.

Sergeant Charles Floyd became very ill, possibly from a ruptured appendix. None of Lewis's or Clark's medical remedies helped him. Floyd died on August 20 and was buried near present-day Sioux City, Iowa. Patrick Gass was elected sergeant in his place.

After they arrived at the James River, seventy Indians appeared on the far bank. These were the Yankton Sioux, one of the seven major groups of the Sioux nation. This council would be good practice for a later meeting with the more aggressive Teton Sioux, who lived farther north.

The soldiers ferried the Indians across the river in the white pirogue, making many trips. The Indians were dressed in their finest clothes—beaded moccasins, high leggings, and buffalo robes. The buffalo robes were worn with the hairy side in. The outward-facing skin side was painted with colorful designs or pictures of the owner's brave deeds. The Indian men wore hawk and eagle feathers in their hair. The women wore deerskin dresses and buffalo robes. Both men's and women's clothing was decorated with feathers, quills, beads, and painted designs.

The council took several days. Lewis gave his speech on the first day, and the Indians replied with speeches on the second day. Communication was imperfect. None of the members of the expedition knew more than a smattering of the Indians' language, and translating was done in sign language. The Yankton Sioux were pleased with the types of gifts they were given, but not with the amount. They told Lewis that they needed more gifts. He replied that he could not spare more because he needed all that was left for trade with other tribes. He assured the Sioux that there would soon be American traders on the river bringing all of the goods that they desired.

The corps traveled on through present-day South Dakota, where the land changed. Trees disappeared and the air became dry. Buffalo grazed on the short grasses of the level plain. Lewis estimated that there were three thousand buffalo grazing within his view. The buffalo, or bison, were gigantic beasts, the largest game animals in North America. The bulls sometimes measured six feet (two meters) tall at the shoulders and weighed around 2,000 pounds (907 kilograms). The cows were much smaller. Many millions of buffalo ranged the Great Plains. Indians depended heavily on the great herds for food, shelter, and clothing.

The men saw many animals that were new to them: jackrabbits, coyotes, mule deer, pronghorn antelope, and prairie dogs. The captains thought that coyotes were a type of fox. After they examined one that had been shot and brought into camp, they decided that it was a small wolf.

The pronghorn antelope were arrestingly beautiful animals. They were small; the males averaged 100 pounds (45 kilograms) and the females weighed less.

Buffalo

Pronghorns were mainly reddish-brown, but their bellies, chests, and portions of their necks were white. Their hooves and noses were black. Both males and females had black horns. Long-legged and fast, they could run up to 60 miles (97 kilometers) an hour. Lewis wrote that their progress was more like "the rapid flight of birds than the motion of quadrupeds."

Pronghorn antelope

The captains were determined to send the president a live prairie dog. Prairie dogs were ground squirrels, named for the distinctive barking sound they used to warn of danger. They lived in large communities and built vast underground mazes of tunnels. They never strayed far from the entrances to their burrows. Always alert to danger, the prairie dogs could not be taken easily by surprise, so the soldiers set to work with shovels to dig one out of its burrow. They dug for hours without luck, until someone thought of pouring water down the burrow. They flushed out a wet, miserable prairie dog that eventually reached the president in Washington.

Lewis also found a huge fossil—the 45-foot (14-meter) skeleton of an ancient reptile—which he included in the growing inventory of items for the president.

The first Teton Sioux they met were three boys, who went back to their village with the explorers' invitation to a council. Two days later, on September 25, 1804, Indians began arriving in their camp in small groups. When Lewis judged that enough had arrived, he gave his speech. Pipes of tobacco were smoked, gifts were given, and food eaten. Nothing impressed these Indians, neither the drills of the uniformed soldiers nor the air gun demonstrations. They accepted their gifts ungraciously.

Prairie dogs

Sioux Indians holding a ceremony to honor the setting sun

Lewis and Clark invited the three chiefs—Partisan, Buffalo Medicine, and head chief Black Buffalo—aboard the keelboat, where they offered them a glass of whiskey. When the chiefs were rowed ashore in one of the pirogues, the Indians seized it and held fast to the rope and the mast. They clearly intended to keep it, along with all of its cargo. Partisan told Clark that the Americans could go no farther up the Missouri. A shouting, shoving match followed. Clark pulled out his sword, the Indians strung their bows with arrows, and Lewis turned the swivel guns toward the Sioux.

A tense moment passed before Black Buffalo ordered the Indians to release the pirogue. Then, surprisingly, both Black Buffalo and Buffalo Medicine asked to travel aboard the keelboat to their village.

Indian village in winter

Lewis and Clark agreed, in hopes of making friends with the Sioux.

The following day, they reached the village, an impressive gathering of eighty tepees. The tepees were large, cone-shaped, and comfortable. Each one was made of twenty or thirty buffalo hides sewn together and draped over a frame of long poles.

The men ate roasted dog meat and pemmican, a mixture of dried meat, fat, and chokecherries. The Sioux danced for the Americans, men and women performing separate dances. Everyone seemed friendly, but the explorers were tense. An Omaha Indian, a prisoner of war in the village, warned Pierre Cruzatte that the Sioux planned to use force to stop the corps from going upriver.

The men slept aboard the boats, which were anchored midstream, and left on September 30. The captains did not feel that they had put the Sioux far enough behind them to risk sending Drouillard and Shields out to hunt. Both of the expedition's horses, which the hunters used to bring the game back to camp, were gone. One had disappeared near the Sioux village and another had been left in Iowa. The men ate pork, meal, and dried soup. The weather grew colder. One morning, frost coated the boats.

In present-day South Dakota, the explorers met the Arikaras. These Indians were fine horsemen. They were so fond of their horses that they brought their best mounts inside their houses at night. Their homes were unlike anything that the explorers had seen yet. They were large, rounded domes with wood-beam frames covered with packed dirt and grass. Each house was roomy enough for a family and its favorite horses. The structures were so sturdy that the Arikaras spent mild evenings lounging and visiting on top of their roofs. The Arikaras grew squash, beans, and corn. They traded their horses and vegetables to the Sioux for buffalo meat and skins.

The Arikaras were very friendly to the explorers. York, who amazed them with his great strength and dark skin, was a general favorite. Clark described the Arikaras as "dirty, poor, kind and extravagant, possessing national pride, not beggarly." The Arikaras refused to drink whiskey. Pleasant as the time spent among the Arikaras was, the men felt they must push on to the Mandan Villages.

The first snow of the season fell on October 21. Winter came early in this region, now North Dakota. When the party finally reached the first of the five

settlements known as the Mandan Villages, the Indians were happy to see them, knowing that they would have trade goods. The Americans, for their part, were equally happy to see the Mandans. It had been their goal to reach the Mandan Villages before winter came and the river froze. It was now October 25, 1804. They were none too soon if they intended to build a winter fort before the harsh northern winter began in earnest.

One of the Mandan villages along the Missouri River

Chapter 5
Fort Mandan

The men badly needed a rest. Colds, infections, and boils were bothering many of them. Clark was suffering from rheumatism. However, the first business on arrival was not rest but an Indian council.

Although the five riverside villages were called the Mandan Villages, the Mandans lived in only the lower two. The other three villages belonged to the Minitaris, allies of the Mandans. Lewis and Clark visited Sheheke and Black Cat, chiefs of the two Mandan villages, and hired three Indian runners to invite the chiefs of the upper villages to a council. The day of the council, October 28, was cold, so the captains had the soldiers put up not only the usual canvas roof but also some canvas walls.

Lewis and Clark entering the Mandan villages

Interior of a Mandan lodge, as drawn by artist Karl Bodmer

The council went well. The Indians had no objections to the corps wintering near them. They were wary, however, about peace promises given by an Arikara chief, since the Arikaras often raided the Mandan Villages. The Arikaras were, in turn, attacked by Sioux raiding parties. The Mandans themselves were a peaceful tribe, but their allies, the Minitaris, raided other tribes, stealing horses and kidnapping women and children. Intertribal warfare was a way of life for the Indians, and nothing that Lewis and Clark could say would change that.

Following the council, the captains found a good site for a fort. It was a wooded, defensible spot, slightly downstream and across the river from the lowest Mandan Village. The party still feared a Sioux attack and were wary of the friendly Mandans, too. The men lived in tents while they built the *V*-shaped fort. It had four rooms along each long arm of the *V* and a large inner courtyard. The rooms had stone fireplaces for heat and cooking. The captains had one room to themselves and everyone else shared the others.

A reconstruction of Fort Mandan

The fort was completed before the end of November. The party had to find food and firewood to last through the bitter winter. They knew that they would be called upon to share food with the Indians when times were hard.

The fort bustled with activity. There was a constant stream of Indian visitors. The Missouri was no obstacle to the Mandans, who often paddled across the river in their round, hide-covered bullboats to see what the soldiers at the fort were doing.

The captains dismissed the French boatmen, since this was as far as they had agreed to go. Some of the Frenchmen went downstream to the Arikara town, while others built a hut outside Fort Mandan's walls. Two Canadian traders and their families set up tepees beside the fort: Rene Jessaume with his Indian wife and young child, and Touissant Charbonneau with his young and pregnant Indian wife, Sacajawea.

Sacajawea was only fifteen or sixteen years old. She was not a Mandan at all, but a Shoshoni who had been captured by a Minitari war party when she was only ten years old. Charbonneau, who had won her in a game, did not treat her kindly. Seeing a chance to make some money, he offered himself to the captains as an interpreter. Knowing that Sacajawea could help them when they encountered the Shoshoni, Lewis and Clark hired Charbonneau. He and Sacajawea would go west with the party when they left in the spring. Another trader, Baptiste LePage, joined the corps.

A Mandan buffalo-hide bullboat

That winter was bitter; the temperature often dropped below zero (−18 degrees Celsius). One day the temperature fell to 45 below zero (−43 degrees Celsius). The Mandans, to the white men's amazement, played lacrosse naked on the frozen river on many of these sub-zero days. The explorers themselves were plagued with frostbite.

Food supplies dwindled. Lewis was reluctant to trade more goods for food, so he had John Shields set up his forge to repair and make tools for the Indians in exchange for food. Chief Sheheke arrived at Fort Mandan one December day in great excitement. The buffalo, he told them, had come down out of the plains and into the river bottom. The Indians were ready for the hunt but were waiting to give the white men a chance also. The men poured out of the fort to join the hunt. The Indians on horseback killed thirty or forty buffalo, but the corps, afoot, killed only ten, five of which they lost to the wolves.

Packs of gray wolves followed the bison, preying on young, old, and sick animals. Scavenging among the carcasses was easy work for the wolves. Lewis, who had observed them hunt, knew that they were intelligent predators. They would pick an animal out from the herd and take turns pursuing it. Using teamwork, they could pursue and kill even the swift pronghorn antelope.

Christmas of 1804 was celebrated with gun salutes, whiskey, and dancing. The Indians had been politely asked not to visit the fort on this "medicine day." The New Year's celebration was a shared event. Sixteen men went across the river to the Mandan village to dance for the Indians, who were delighted by the jigs and especially by York's spirited cavorting.

The explorers had nothing but dried vegetables to eat by February. Lewis wrote on February 4: "Our stock of meat which we had procured in the months of November and December is now nearly exhausted. . . . No buffalo have made their appearance in our neighborhood for some weeks."

Clark and a group of hunters left Fort Mandan to find meat. They killed a number of buffalo and cached the meat in log cribs that they built. When Drouillard and several other men returned for the meat with horses and sleighs, they were attacked by over one hundred Sioux warriors, who took two of their horses. Drouillard ordered his men not to shoot, and the Sioux, who had no guns, did not harm them. The Sioux brought the meat back later, but it was clear that they were hostile to the corps. They had, in fact, declared war on the expedition in November. Winter weather had made them postpone plans for an attack. The explorers would not be safe once spring arrived.

Sacajawea gave birth to a son in February 1805. The baby was named Jean Baptiste, but Sacajawea usually called her son Pomp. So did Clark, who became very fond of the little boy and of his mother.

Over the winter, the boats became locked in ice that was many feet thick. They could be crushed when the ice broke up in the spring. To prevent this, the men broke the boats free with iron levers and dragged them up on the shore with ropes. When the ice finally broke, many buffalo were trapped on huge ice cakes and carried downriver, bellowing. Indians leapt from floe to floe to reach the stranded buffalo and kill them. They then paddled the ice chunks with the dead buffalo on them to shore. They also dragged the floating carcasses of dead buffalo to shore with ropes.

Monticello, the Virginia home of Thomas Jefferson

At last the river was open again, and the captains made plans to depart. The corps left Fort Mandan on April 7, 1805. First they said good-bye to Corporal Warfington, who departed downriver in the keelboat with his soldiers and several French rivermen. The boat was packed with articles for President Jefferson: seed, soil samples, plants, Indian pottery, bones, furs, horns, insects, and buffalo robes. There were live animals, too, including five magpies, a grouse, and a prairie dog.

The captains included bundles of papers and reports containing all of their notes on the Indians—their numbers, languages, and customs. Clark sent a detailed report on all the rivers and streams they had seen. He had spent the winter gathering information about the Western lands from the Minitaris, who rode as far as the Rocky Mountains in war parties. Lewis added his own shrewd, detailed observations of nature. He had written about everything from the total eclipse of the moon to the hunting habits of wolves. Jefferson would be interested in all of it.

Corporal Warfington eventually reached the port of New Orleans. From there, the shipment went overland to Washington, D.C., reaching the capital while Jefferson was at home in Monticello. The servants made the magpies and the prairie dog comfortable in one of the rooms of the White House until Jefferson's return.

The president sent the animals and many of the objects in the shipment to Peale's Natural History Museum in Philadelphia. The seeds were sent through a naturalist society to plant nurserymen all over the United States. Jefferson kept many of the Indian artifacts at Monticello.

With the keelboat shrinking in the distance, the corps boarded their own fleet, the two pirogues and six dugouts. In March, the men had carved the dugouts from the trunks of huge cottonwood trees. Charbonneau, Sacajawea, and Pomp joined the captains in the white pirogue. In all, there were thirty-three people and a dog.

No one in the boats realized it at the time, but their prompt departure had saved them from the Sioux, who were planning to attack. Leaving that danger behind, they paddled on into the far reaches of the high plains.

Cottonwood tree

Chapter 6
The High Plains

Charbonneau and LePage had ventured up the Missouri beyond the Mandan Villages several times in the past. Within a week, the Lewis and Clark party reached a large island that Charbonneau and LePage recognized. This was as far as they or any other white man had ever come upriver. Beyond that point lay country that only the Indians knew.

The high plains were home to huge herds of buffalo, deer, elk, and antelope. Flocks of geese and ducks flew overhead. The corps passed thriving beaver colonies. None of the animals or birds were alarmed at their passing. Buffalo and elk came down to the riverbank to gaze curiously as the boats passed. At one campsite, a buffalo calf adopted Lewis and followed him until it was time for the party to board the boats and leave.

At the end of April the travelers passed the mouth of the Yellowstone River and entered the present-day state of Montana. They were alert for signs of grizzly bears. Over the winter, they had heard Indian tales of the fierce "white bears." Grizzlies were not actually white at all. Their coats were usually gray or yellowish-tan, but their hair was tipped in a lighter silver or white color, which gave them a grizzled appearance. So fearsome were these bears that any warrior who killed one earned great respect in the tribe. Grizzly bear talons were a prized possession.

Lewis believed that the grizzlies were probably dangerous foes to Indians armed only with bows and arrows. But he thought they would prove no match at all for men with rifles. On May 14, six men spotted a large bear napping not far from the river. Though the grizzly was not threatening them, they decided to kill it. Leaving the dugouts, they crept up on the sleeping bear. Four of them shot at the animal, which immediately charged. Then the other two hunters fired.

Despite its wounds, the bear moved fast. The hunters had no time to reload their guns. The bear singled out two men, and by the time they sprinted to the river, the bear was right at their heels. Terrified, the men jumped down a twenty-foot (six-meter) bank into the river. The bear plunged in, too. He was only a few feet behind one of the men when a hunter on shore managed to kill it with a shot to the head. After this, everyone had great respect for the hulking, solitary bears. Lewis commented only that "the curiosity of our party is pretty well satisfied with respect to this animal."

The white pirogue was the best boat that the expedition had now, so it carried the most important

Grizzly bear

This picture by expedition member Patrick Gass shows Lewis and Clark losing many of their notes and specimens when their canoe overturned on the return trip.

supplies. It also carried Drouillard (when he was not hunting), Lewis (when he was not walking ashore), Clark, Charbonneau, Sacajawea, and Pomp.

In mid-May, Charbonneau almost capsized the white pirogue. Both captains were on shore at the time. Cruzatte asked Charbonneau to hold the helm for only a moment. The trader lost hold of the helm in a sudden gust of wind, and the pirogue heeled over on its side. The sails were now wet and the boat was rapidly filling with water. Charbonneau panicked and began shouting and praying. Cruzatte brought Charbonneau to his senses by threatening to shoot him. Charbonneau began to steer again, at gunpoint. Cruzatte ordered two men to bail water with kettles, while he and others rowed the crippled boat ashore.

There were times when the men had to tow the boats for an entire day. They bruised their feet on sharp rocks and cut them on the sharp spines of the prickly-pear cactus. Rattlesnakes slithered away at their approach.

On May 19, Seaman was bitten by a beaver and nearly bled to death. There was another close call when a confused buffalo blundered into the party's camp at night, coming within inches of trampling some of the sleepers.

The captains named rivers and creeks: Milk River, Brown Bear Defeated Creek, Burnt Lodge Creek. Some of the names are the same today, while others have changed. Clark named the Judith River for Julia Hancock. When the party passed the remains of a buffalo herd that the Indians had stampeded off a cliff, the captains called the place Slaughter Creek.

Judith River, Montana

On June 3, the corps hit an unexpected fork in the river. The Indians had not warned them about it. They were unsure of which way to go and had no time to lose on a wrong choice if they were to cross the mountains before the autumn snows. Both forks were of equal size. The soldiers favored the north branch because it was as muddy as the Missouri had been all along. The captains liked the looks of the clear southern fork, which appeared to lead toward the mountains. The captains decided to scout both forks carefully. Clark and several men explored the southern fork, while Lewis and his men went up the northern fork. When all had returned to camp, the captains were of one mind. The southern fork was the Missouri. They felt that it led to the mountains, while the northern fork went off into the plains. Lewis named the northern fork Marias River in honor of a woman he liked.

The men were uneasy with the captains' decision. To calm all doubts, Lewis decided to travel ahead and look for the Great Falls of the Missouri, of which the Indians had spoken. Once they found the falls, everyone would know that they were still on the Missouri.

The southern fork was so swift and shallow that the party left behind some heavy baggage and the red pirogue. They dug a deep, dry pit and cached the boat, tools, food, and ammunition. Lewis took three men with him and continued on. On June 13, they heard a constant thundering ahead and saw rising mist. The Great Falls! Lewis was so amazed by the beauty of the scene that he sat and watched for four hours. The waters of the Missouri cascaded over an 80-foot (24-meter) drop, crashing into foam below. A rainbow hovered overhead. Lewis wrote that it was the "grandest sight I ever beheld."

Marias River, Montana

The Great Falls of the Missouri

Beautiful though it was, the Great Falls was a major obstacle to the party. There were five separate falls before the next stretch of navigable river.

Lewis sent Joseph Fields back to the boats with the news that Great Falls had been found. He himself went on to the end of the falls, where he planned to camp alone for the night. His eye fell upon a buffalo standing handily within range of his gun, and he thought it would provide a fine dinner. No sooner had Lewis shot the buffalo than he discovered he was being stalked by a large grizzly. His gun was empty and the closest tree was a good 300 yards (274 meters) away. As Lewis started for the tree, the bear charged. Realizing that he would not reach the tree in time, Lewis veered to the nearby river and jumped down

A North American cougar

the bank. Standing in the waist-high water, he turned to face the bear, holding his steel-tipped staff in front of him. The bear was surprised when Lewis turned to confront him. Miraculously, the grizzly fled.

Lewis's troubles were not over. Returning to claim the dead buffalo, he saw a big cat that "couched itself down . . . to spring on me." Lewis fired at the cat, which disappeared into its burrow. This "tiger cat" was probably a cougar. "It now seemed to me that all of the beasts of the neighborhood had made a league to destroy me," he wrote. The next challenge came from three bull buffalo who ran at him, stopped 100 yards (91 meters) away, and then retreated. Lewis decided to forget his buffalo, feeling that it was not "prudent to remain all night at this place."

Lewis returned to the boats, which had stopped a safe five miles (eight kilometers) above the first of the falls, by a stream the captains dubbed Portage Creek. Clark and the main group had reached Portage Creek after two days of boat travel. Clark worried constantly about Sacajawea, who had fallen ill and was getting worse by the day. Delirious with pain, she lay with her baby in the bottom of the white pirogue under a sailcloth awning. Clark believed that "her case is somewhat dangerous." If Sacajawea should die, he worried, who would care for the infant Pomp? Would the captains be able to procure horses from the Shoshoni without Sacajawea?

When Lewis returned to camp, Sacajawea was still desperately ill. Clark had bled her repeatedly, but

Page from William Clark's journal, with his drawing of a trout

this had not helped her at all. He had applied poultices made of bark, water, and flour to her abdomen. Lewis, seeing her condition, decided to try some new treatments. He gave Sacajawea some opium and water from a nearby spring. By June 17, the captains were relieved to see that Sacajawea was "free from pain, clear of fever."

That same day, Clark went out to mark a portage trail with wooden stakes. The shortest route around the falls was 18 miles (29 kilometers), a long way for the men to carry all of the boats and baggage. The men located a single large cottonwood tree in the area and used its wood to build two wagons. Next, they fitted the wagons with sails in hopes of catching any breeze that might help them.

Portaging around rough waters

Clark and eighteen men handled the portage, making trip after trip with the heavily laden wagons. The soft cottonwood wheels broke and new wheels had to be built with whatever wood was at hand. It was the hardest physical work of the trip so far. High winds blew sand in the men's eyes. Heavy rain fell, and there was one violent hailstorm.

At the end of the long portage, the party camped on White Bear Island, where Lewis acted as cook. York, Charbonneau, and Sacajawea manned the camp back at Portage Creek. Food was always ready at both camps to feed the hungry workers. Drouillard and others hunted game to keep the cooking kettles full.

One day, the ground was so slick with rain that all portaging stopped. Clark was with Charbonneau, Sacajawea, and Pomp. A high wind forced them to retreat into a little ravine. The ravine, dry one moment, was suddenly filled with rising water from a flash flood. Charbonneau scrambled out and began to pull Sacajawea and Pomp to safety. Then terror gripped him and he froze. Clark pushed Sacajawea and her baby up out of the ravine to safety and climbed free himself, but not before he was in water up to his waist. It had been a very close call. Sacajawea lost Pomp's carrier and some of his clothes. Clark lost an umbrella, a powder horn, and a large compass.

More than a month was spent getting around Great Falls. Lewis first saw the falls on June 13, and the party was not on its way again until July 15. Lewis wrote, "I begin to be extremely impatient . . . nearly three months have now elapsed since we left Fort Mandan and not yet reached the Rocky Mountains."

They needed to replace the red pirogue, which was cached by the Marias River. Lewis counted heavily on

Lewis and Clark named this spot along the Missouri's course Gates of the Mountains.

using the collapsible, iron-framed boat that he had designed. The hunters produced enough elk skins to cover the frame. It took some time to assemble the *Experiment*, as Lewis called the boat.

On July 9, the finished *Experiment* was set in the water where, as Lewis wrote, "It lay like a perfect cork." Not for long, however, because a sudden storm blew up. Before the storm was over, the *Experiment* was taking in water through every seam in the elk hides. Lewis was bitterly disappointed.

Lewis went fishing while Clark went off with some men to find trees large enough to carve two more dugouts. Six day later, they had finished and were on their way in eight dugouts.

Crossing the mountains was the next concern. The explorers had first seen the distant snow-covered peaks in early June. The closer they got, the more formidable the mountains appeared.

They were nearing the Continental Divide. The rivers on one side of the divide flowed east, while those on the other side flowed west. President Jefferson hoped that there was a short and easy portage from the eastward-flowing Missouri River to the westward-flowing Columbia or one of its tributaries. Lewis and Clark, gazing at the majestic Rocky Mountain range, had reason to doubt this. It did not look as though there would be any easy way to cross those moun-

The Lewis and Clark expedition's first view of the Rocky Mountains

tains, either by water or on foot. The trek from the Missouri to the Columbia was not going to be easy. They were going to need horses.

They had to find the Shoshoni Indians, who had many horses. Clark, York, and some others went ahead on foot to look for them. They found recent trails but no Indians. By July 25, the scouts reached Three Forks, where the Missouri split into three smaller rivers. Sacajawea recognized Three Forks as the place where she had been kidnapped many years before. The captains named the three rivers the Gallatin (after the secretary of the treasury), the Madison, and the Jefferson.

Lewis, Clark, and Sacajawea at the Three Forks of the Missouri

They took the Jefferson because it led into the mountains. Some distance upstream, the Jefferson split into several forks. Above the forks, the Jefferson has become known as the Beaverhead River. Lewis went ahead to look for the Shoshoni. On August 11, he spotted a horseback Indian in the distance. The Indian had seen them, too. Lewis took a blanket, lifted it above his head, and spread it on the ground. It was a sign of friendship among the Plains Indians, a way of inviting a guest to sit on a blanket and talk. He did this three times, but the wary Indian scout kept his distance. Then Lewis dug gifts out of his pack and walked toward the Shoshoni, holding them out and repeating the word "Tab-ba-bone." Lewis thought the

Lewis and Clark trying to make friends with the Indians

Lewis Rock near Three Forks

word meant friend, but it meant stranger. Lewis had signalled his men to halt, but Shields, off to one side, had not seen the signal and plodded ahead with a rifle in hand. The Shoshoni feared a trap, turned his horse's head, and was gone in an instant. Irate, Lewis tongue-lashed Shields, but it was too late.

Two days later, Lewis finally met three Indian women. They expected to be killed and were thrilled to receive gifts instead. The women led the men toward their village, but before they arrived, the explorers were surrounded by sixty mounted warriors, painted for war. When they understood the strangers were friendly, they embraced them, cheek to cheek.

Wilderness area near where Lewis and Clark met the Shoshoni

The Shoshoni were a poor tribe, always close to starvation. Although they had many horses, they had no guns, as did their enemies the Minitaris, Crows, and Blackfeet. These peoples chased the Shoshoni into the foothills of the mountains, where they often found nothing but roots and berries to eat. Lewis smoked with Chief Cameahwait, and he and his men camped with the Indians overnight. The Indians shared their only food, berries, with the white men.

Lewis coaxed Cameahwait and his people to the river where they could see the trade goods. Then they might be willing to trade their horses. When they reached the riverbank, there were no boats in sight. The Indians were nervous. Lewis promised that, if they stayed, they would soon see wonderful sights: a black man, and a Shoshoni woman who had been

This monument to Sacajawea in Bismarck, North Dakota, was sculpted by Leonard Crunelle. The schoolchildren and women's clubs of the state raised money for it.

stolen from the tribe long ago. He offered beads and a knife to any Indian brave enough to go with Drouillard to meet the boats. Several warriors took the challenge. The following day, the Indians who had left with Drouillard returned. They shouted that the boats were coming. All that Lewis had said was true. They had seen both the black man and the Shoshoni woman.

As the boats arrived, Sacajawea danced with joy at the sight of her own people. Clark was brought to Lewis and Cameahwait. The chief placed six small seashells in Clark's hair, and the three men shared a pipe. When Sacajawea and Charbonneau were summoned to help translate, Sacajawea recognized Cameahwait as her brother. Weeping, she rose and covered his head with her blanket. Cameahwait wept with her. Sacajawea had found her long-lost family.

Chapter 7
Across the Rockies
and Beyond

The Shoshoni wanted rifles more than any of the things that Lewis and Clark offered. Much as the explorers needed horses, they could not spare any rifles in trade for them. Cameahwait told the captains, "If we had guns we would then live in the country of buffalo and eat as our enemies do and not be compelled to hide ourselves in these mountains and live on roots and berries as the bears do." Lewis and Clark could only promise that traders would follow them. Guns would be available—in a couple of years.

Clark left the horse-trading to Lewis and went to the Shoshoni village. There he talked with an old man who told Clark that river travel was impossible but that there was an overland trail. The Nez Perce, or Pierced Nose, Indians who lived on the other side of the mountains used this trail. It was difficult and there was no food along the way.

Clark was still hoping that there was a way to go on by boat. He hired a guide called Old Toby to take him a short distance into the mountains. When Old Toby showed him the wild water where the Lehmi and Salmon rivers met, Clark knew that they would have to take the overland trail.

Lewis was not having much luck buying horses. He had fewer than a dozen. The Shoshoni were gathering to descend to the plains and hunt buffalo. They were unwilling to part with horses before the hunt. Lewis felt that he would do better at the Shoshoni village, where there would be horses not needed in the buffalo hunt.

Horses or not, the party had saddles. The men had been busy making some out of packing cases and the blades of oars. Many supplies had been cached by the Jefferson-Beaverhead River. What was left was loaded on the horses or shouldered by the soldiers and some Indian women who had been hired as porters.

Cameahwait was torn. His tribe had lost many horses in a recent raid. His people would ask high prices for the ones that were left. Without his aid, the captains stood little chance of getting the mounts that they needed to cross the mountains. If he returned to the village to help Lewis, perhaps his people would have guns in the future. But returning to the village meant postponing the buffalo hunt, and the Shoshoni needed meat for the long winter. It was a dilemma.

The chief decided to return to his village with Lewis. On the way, the travelers actually crossed the Continental Divide at Lehmi Pass. The captains spent several days in hard bargaining. Although they had wanted fifty-five horses, they had to settle for twenty-nine. Most of the men would have to walk.

On August 30, the village emptied out. The Indians hurried south to hunt buffalo, while the Lewis and Clark party traveled north along the Salmon River. Old Toby and one of his sons agreed to guide them across the Bitterroot Mountains, a part of the Rocky Mountain chain.

They toiled up and down steep hills, the horses slipping and sometimes falling. Early snow fell. Everyone was cold, wet, and hungry. The only game they saw was an occasional grouse, so they ate pork rations. Clark thought that these were "some of the worst roads that a horse ever passed." This was known as the Lost Trail. It was only the first leg of their mountain crossing.

Indians sneaking up on buffalo by disguising themselves under pelts

Montana's Bitterroot River

After a week of hard travel, they descended into a pleasant valley, which they named Traveller's Rest. Here by the banks of the Bitterroot River lived the Flathead Indians. They offered the party roots to eat and sold them a dozen good horses. Neither group had time for an extended visit. The Flatheads were impatient to take the Lost Trail to the buffalo hunt, and the explorers wanted to move on.

The toughest segment of the crossing lay ahead. It has become known as the Lolo Trail. Talking with Old Toby, Clark discovered how close they had been to the Lolo Trail before, when they were at Great Falls. The guide pointed out a pass that led back over the Continental Divide. Just beyond the pass, he said, was Great Falls. The expedition had come more than 500

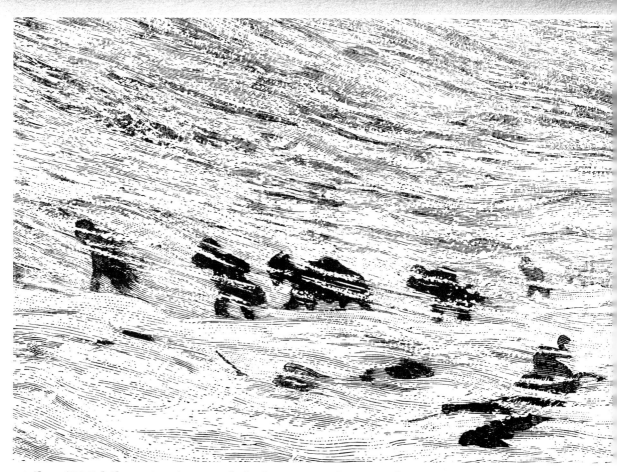

Trekking through a blizzard

miles (805 kilometers) out of their way, going south and then north in a large loop to find the Shoshoni. They had had no choice. Without horses, they could never have crossed the mountains.

They started up the Lolo Trail on September 11, riding into an early snow. Toby lost his way, and it took time to get back on the trail. Progress was slow. They inched their way up and down steep, rocky ridges, where sharp rocks cut the horses' legs. The mountain air was so thin that the men were exhausted. Several mornings they woke up covered with snow. Hunger knotted their stomachs. Lewis's portable soup was all that they had for several days. They resorted to killing and eating the three half-grown colts that accompanied mares. They were still hungry.

Clark and six men went ahead to find meat and managed to shoot a lost Indian horse. Lewis and the others struggled on through the mountains, half-starved and ill. One night they dined on soup, bear oil, and candle wax. Another night, they ate a slightly better meal of three grouse, one coyote, and some crayfish, divided among the twenty-eight of them. Not until September 22 did they descend the Lolo Trail to the plains. Clark met them with food and the welcome news that they were only a day's travel from a branch of the Columbia River. The Rockies were behind them.

They set up Canoe Camp by the Clearwater River, a branch of the Columbia. During the next eleven days, they burned and hollowed five dugouts. Twisted Hair, a Nez Perce chief, agreed to care for their thirty-eight horses until they returned. Twisted Hair himself and a chief called Tetoharsky would guide them through Nez Perce country. On October 7, the corps broke camp and headed with the current down the Clearwater.

The Clearwater carried them through the rugged foothills of the Rockies. The land about them, present-day Idaho, was harsh and rocky. Lewis had noted that the Nez Perce had little time for recreation because they had to spend so much time finding food. Indian men hunted game and fished for salmon; the women dug for the roots of the camas lily, which they used to make both soup and bread. The Nez Perce were excellent horsemen and hunters. The captains liked them.

Old Toby and his son left for home one day without a word to anyone. The corps entered a new geographical region, the Columbian Plain. It was a cold and barren desert—a rocky, windswept land where even Drouillard could not find any game. There were

Lewis and Clark at the mouth of the Columbia River

no trees in this dry region, so the corps bought small bundles of firewood from the local Nez Perce Indians.

The Clearwater ran into the Snake River, a much larger stream. Four days of travel brought them to the junction of the Snake and the Columbia rivers, a favorite fishing site of the Indians. They stopped to rest and to meet the Indians gathered on the shore. These were the Yakima Indians, a people closely related to the Nez Perce. They lived in rectangular houses made of woven rush mats and poles. The captains held a short council and gave gifts. Several hundred Indian men danced to the beat of drums for the entertainment of the corps. Lewis and Clark purchased food, passing over the salmon, which seemed spoiled to them, and buying forty dogs for meat instead.

Indians catching salmon on the Columbia River

Salmon was the mainstay of the Indian diet from here to the Pacific Ocean. The salmon run was just ending, and dead salmon floated on the surface of the river. Each year from April until October, the salmon returned from the sea, swimming upstream to reach their spawning grounds. Indians gathered to snare the fish with spears and nets. The shores were lined with large wooden racks where the fish were dried.

The party continued on, riding the Columbia River through a bleak land of rocky canyons. They discovered that the Columbia had its share of hazards for travelers. At Celilo Falls, the river fell 80 feet (24 meters) in a several-mile run. Dugouts and baggage were portaged around the worst of the falls. The empty dugouts rode through some of the smaller falls. Celilo Falls was only the first of many rough spots.

The river cut through the Cascade Mountains, the last mountain range standing between the corps and the Pacific Ocean. Neither as high nor as wide as the Rockies, the Cascades were thickly forested with evergreens. Going through the mountains, the Columbia was forced into tight channels where the water pounded and surged dangerously. There were two such spots—the Long Narrows and the Short Narrows. Once the corps passed these obstacles, Twisted Hair and Tetoharsky left them.

The climate changed abruptly on the western side of the Cascades. The air was humid and rain fell almost every day. In the mornings, the river was shrouded in mist. The shores were a tangle of vegetation. They maneuvered through the upper and lower Cascades, two dangerous stretches of white water.

Clark's map of the great falls of the Columbia River, showing many islands and a portage route

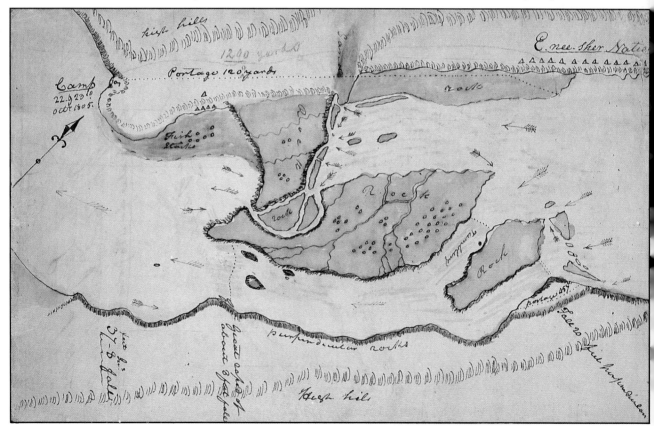

The Lewis and Clark expedition encounters Chinook Indians on the Columbia River; Sacajawea speaks to them in sign language. Painting by Charles M. Russell

The peoples that they met next were Chinooks. There were different tribes among the Chinooks: Wishrams, Skilloots, Clatsops, and others. Salmon was the staple of the Chinook diet. Their houses were made of wooden planks, and several families often lived in one house. The Chinooks bound their infants' heads between boards to mold them into the elongated and pointed shape that they considered beautiful. They also pierced their noses with small, curved seashells.

The explorers came to distrust the Chinooks because they stole things from the party whenever they were able. Some of the Chinooks that they met were afraid of the white men until they saw Sacajawea.

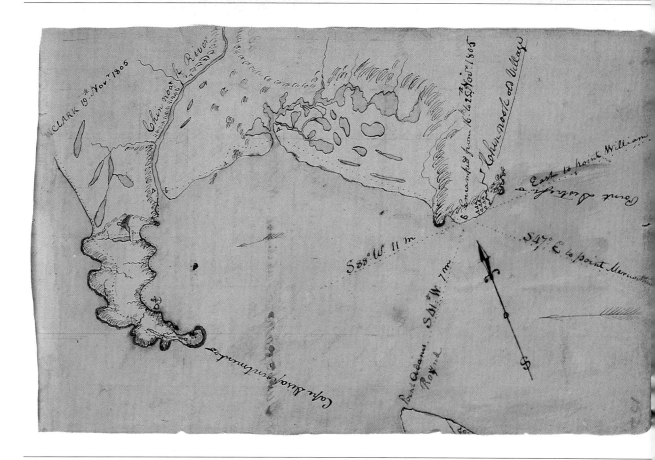

Clark's map showing lands around the mouth of the Columbia River

The presence of a woman reassured them that this was not a war party.

The corps rejoiced on November 7, 1805, believing that they had reached the Pacific Ocean. The celebration was premature. They had reached Gray's Bay, but the actual Pacific was still 20 miles (32 kilometers) away. Heavy seas and gale-force winds kept the corps from reaching the ocean for another week. It seemed to the battered corps that a continual storm raged at the mouth of the Columbia River. Heavy rain fell, and waves hurled huge logs at their dugouts. It was difficult to find any level camping ground out of the reach of the tide. They were living on dried, pounded fish and roots.

Pacific surf on the Oregon coast

Lewis reached the ocean first, arriving on November 14 or 15. Clark got there afoot with a larger group on November 18. They were awed by the endless expanse of gray, rolling water. Neither captain spotted a ship, and their hopes for a ride home faded. The party lingered for several weeks at the stormy mouth of the Columbia, but bad weather and poor food convinced them that they could stay no longer. They chose a winter campsite by a small river south of the Columbia, in present-day Oregon.

The site was on a slight rise in a wooded and swampy area teeming with elk. The men cleared the land of trees and brush and built Fort Clatsop. It was a large square with rooms facing each other along each side. Lewis and Clark had their own room, as did Charbonneau, Sacajawea, and Pomp. That left five rooms for everyone else and all of the supplies.

The winter at Fort Clatsop was monotonous. One rainy, gray, chilly day followed the next. Their diet was poor. The meat of the local elk was lean and stringy. Other than elk, they ate roots. They set up a camp by the ocean, where they boiled ocean water in five large kettles to extract the salt. The flavor of meat and roots improved with a sprinkling of sea salt.

In January 1806, they heard that a whale had been beached nearby. Clark hurried to the shore with twelve men and Sacajawea, who had pleaded to be included. He was too late. The Tillamook Indians had arrived first and stripped the whale so thoroughly that only a huge skeleton remained. Clark was able to buy 300 pounds (136 kilograms) of blubber and several gallons of oil at a price that he grumbled was too high. Lewis wrote that the blubber "was very palatable and tender. It resembled the beaver or the dog in flavor."

Fort Clatsop

Lewis and Clark spent the long hours in Fort Clatsop writing their journals. Not since Fort Mandan had they had so much time to write. Lewis finished his excellent, detailed descriptions of plants and animals. Clark completed the map that he had begun at Fort Mandan.

Everyone wanted to go home, but the timing was critical. They couldn't cross the mountains until the snow melted. If they waited too long, the Missouri would freeze and they would have to spend another winter on the Great Plains.

There were three remaining dugouts, but the expedition was still short of boats. Drouillard purchased one canoe with Lewis's fancy dress military coat. Unable to buy another canoe, the explorers stole one from the nearest Clatsop village. They left Fort Clatsop on March 23, 1806, happy to be going home.

One of Lewis's journal pages, with his drawing of a bird

Chapter 8
Homeward Bound

Maneuvering the falls and narrows of the Columbia River had been difficult enough in the autumn. On the return trip, the current was against them and the Columbia was swollen with melted snow. They portaged around the lower Cascades in pouring rain. They were harassed by Chinooks who shouted insults, threw rocks, and tried to jostle them off the narrow, rain-slick portage trail.

The captains posted men to guard the baggage, but the Indians managed to steal some items. Several Chinooks lured Seaman away. Lewis was infuriated by the loss of his pet. He sent three armed men in search of the dog with orders to shoot if they must. Luckily, the Indians gave up the black Newfoundland without a struggle.

At the Upper Cascades, the corps lost a dugout. They were towing it when it turned broadside to the current. The strong current pulled the rope out of the men's hands, and the empty dugout was smashed to pieces on the sharp rocks. Lewis bought two small canoes with some elk skins at the next Indian town.

The captains wanted horses to portage around the Narrows and Celilo Falls. The Indians were unwilling to sell them any. Frustrated, Clark offered his abilities as a "medicine man" in exchange for horses. He treated one old chief for sores and his wife for backache in exchange for a promise of two horses. After several days of hard bargaining, the corps had only that promise and three sorry nags.

The heavy dugouts had to be abandoned at the bottom of Celilo Falls. The captains tried unsuccessfully to sell them to the Indians. When there were no buyers, Lewis ordered the men to chop up the dugouts for firewood. They had more luck selling several canoes for beads that would be useful for later trade.

On April 19, the corps reached the top of Celilo Falls just as the salmon run began. Clark was able to collect on his promise of two horses. The explorers brought their herd up to ten by parting with most of their iron kettles.

More things were stolen. Lewis threatened the Indians, telling them that the explorers could easily kill them if they wished. He beat one Indian who was caught rummaging through the baggage. Everyone was on edge. Lewis described the Indians as "poor, dirty, haughty, inhospitable, parsimonious and faithless in every respect."

On April 21, they continued on. Four men handled the two canoes. The rest marched ashore with the ten

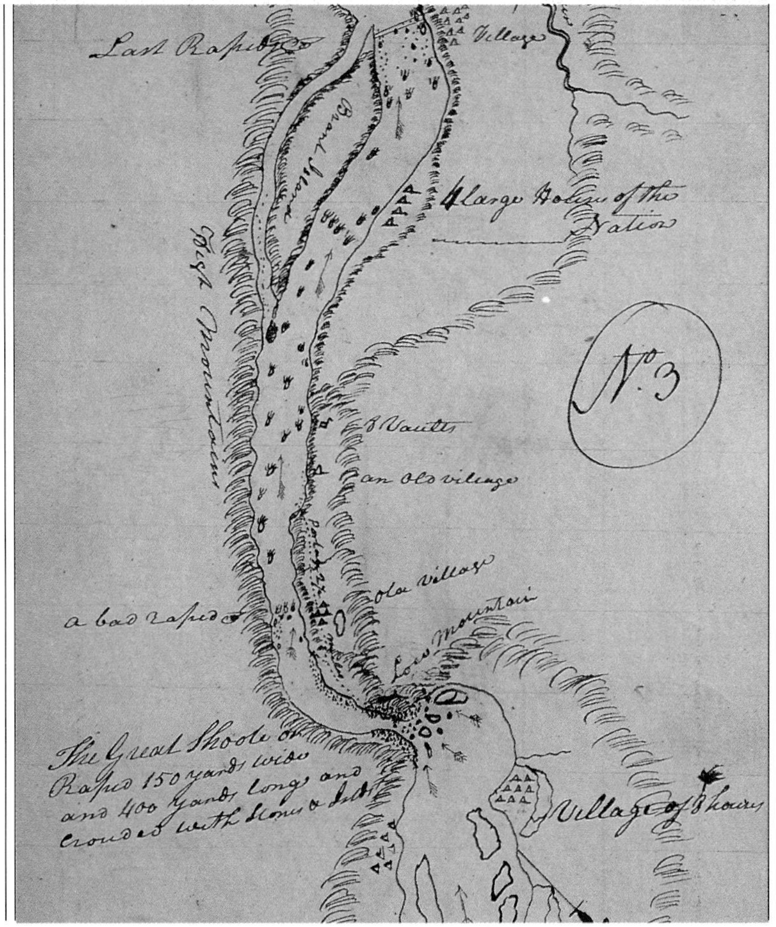

Last Rapid

Village

large House of the Nation

Ns 3

8 Vaults

an old village

old village

Low Mountain

a bad rapid

The Great Shoote or Rapid 150 yards wide and 400 yards long and crowded with stone &c

Village of 8 houses

Clark's map of the great rapids of the Columbia River, showing several Indian villages

heavily packed horses. They continued to barter with groups of Indians who were on their way to the salmon catch. Soon they had enough animals so that none of the men had to carry baggage. They sold their remaining canoes for more beads.

They planned to save some miles taking an overland shortcut instead of following the Clearwater and Snake Rivers north in a long arc. To take the shorter route, they had to cross the Columbia. On April 27, they came upon Yellept, chief of the Walla Walla tribe. They had met him on the trip west but had not had time to stop. Yellept agreed to ferry them across the river after they visited his village. He wished them to meet his own people and the neighboring Yakimas.

Yellept generously gave the party firewood and dogs. He presented the captains with a beautiful white horse. Clark gave Yellept an ornate sword and some bullets. Clark estimated that there were 350 Indian men, women, and children at the gathering in Yellept's village. The explorers performed a jig for the Indians, and the Indians danced for the corps. Some of the men joined in the Indian dance, which pleased the Walla Wallas and Yakimas greatly. The dancing lasted until ten o'clock at night.

The next day, Yellept provided canoes to take the corps to the other side of the river. The twenty-three horses swam across. The captains thanked Yellept and left with warm feelings for the Walla Wallas, "the most hospitable, honest, and sincere people that we have met with on our voyage."

Mount Hood National Forest in northwestern Oregon

By May 3, they had arrived in the land of the Nez Perce again. They were received coolly in Twisted Hair's village. Twisted Hair was quarreling with another chief, Cut Nose, over the care of the explorers' horses. Two chiefs, Cut Nose and Broken Arm, had been jealous that the captains had left their horses with Twisted Hair. Twisted Hair had allowed these two to use the explorers' horses. Now the horses were widely scattered, and Cut Nose was accusing Twisted Hair of negligence in caring for the herd.

Twisted Hair, as it turned out, had not done such a bad job. He had saved most of the expedition's saddles from being ruined when a flood threatened their cache. He received two guns and some ammunition for his services. Most of the straying horses were rounded up quickly. Others were brought back in the next several weeks. Before the expedition crossed the mountains, every horse had been returned—except for two that Old Toby and his son had taken on their trip home.

The expedition visited the village of Chief Broken Arm. His village of fifty families lived in one huge house made of sticks and dried grass. The Indians erected a tepee for Lewis and Clark and gave the corps roots and horse meat. The Nez Perce did not eat dog meat and thought it a strange and repulsive thing to do. A tense moment occurred when one Indian tossed a small puppy on Lewis's plate as a joke. Angry, Lewis threw the puppy back in the man's face. Luckily, that was the end of the incident.

Otherwise, the party enjoyed good relations with the Nez Perce. Broken Arm cautioned the captains against trying to cross the mountains any earlier than the middle of June. Lewis and Clark settled down to wait in a camp some distance away from the village.

Horses, introduced to the North American Indians in the 1700s, enabled them to travel and hunt more efficiently. This picture, by Karl Bodmer, shows a Blackfoot Indian on horseback.

Many of their new horses were fine animals. The Nez Perce loved horses and had bred a new strain of horse—the Appaloosa. The Appaloosas were on the small side but hardy and fast. They were primarily white or brown but covered with small round spots of white or another color. Not all of the corps' new horses were gentle, so the men spent time breaking them. They ate the horses that were too wild to be broken.

It was not long before the area was overhunted. They left on June 10, without the Indian guides that Broken Arm had promised. Each person was riding a horse and leading another. They climbed out of the valley of the Clearwater River to Wieppe Plain, where they stopped to hunt. On June 15, they headed up the Lolo Trail.

It had been spring on the plain, but it was winter in the mountains. They were soon traveling in 8 to 10 feet (2 to 3 meters) of snow. It was packed so hard that it supported the weight of the horses. The real problem was that snow covered the notches they had cut into the pines the previous fall to mark the way. Unable to find their trail, they retreated reluctantly back down the mountain. Drouillard and Shannon returned to the Nez Perce village to promise a gun to anyone who would guide them over the mountains.

Two young Nez Perce warriors happened across the camp and were persuaded to stay. Drouillard and Shannon returned with three other guides. That night the Indians set a copse of pine trees ablaze in a ceremony that they said would guarantee good weather.

The guides led them up the Lolo Trail again. The horses picked their way along the snowy ridges. Hunger marked the mountain crossing again. At one point, they had nothing to eat but bear oil.

Their Indian guides never hesitated. Clark remarked that "These fellows are the most admirable pilots." On June 29, the Nez Perce led them to a hot spring that the Indians used. Everyone enjoyed a warm bath, the first in many months. The Indians ran between the ice-cold creek and the steamy spring water, plunging into one and then the other. Joseph Fields shot a deer, the only fresh meat they had had in days.

On June 30, they reached Traveller's Rest. The crossing had taken only six days! Lewis and Clark planned to part ways here. Lewis and his men would explore the Marias River, which lay to the north. Clark and his group would go south and investigate the Yellowstone. They planned to meet again where the Yellowstone River joined the Missouri.

Chapter 9
Journey's End

L ewis and his group of nine men broke camp on July 3, following the Big Blackfoot River eastward. The five Nez Perce guides had come along to show them a pass over the Continental Divide. Lewis wanted the Indians to cross with them, but the guides were afraid to enter Blackfoot territory. Lewis gave them the rifles they had earned and meat for their trip home.

The explorers went on alone, crossing the Great Divide through a pass now called the Lewis and Clark Pass. They emerged from the mountains near Great Falls. By July 11, they reached White Bear Island. The men opened the cache of goods they had left there. Most of the contents were in good condition, although some skins and plant specimens had rotted.

Here, Lewis split his group into two. He, Drouillard, and the Fields brothers went north to investigate the course of the Marias River. Lewis ordered the rest of the men to portage the supplies around Great Falls to Portage Creek. They were to find and refit the white pirogue that had been left there. If all went according to plan, the men on White Bear Island would soon be joined by some of Clark's men.

The Blackfoot Indians had the reputation of being bloodthirsty. Lewis, Drouillard, and the Fields brothers were on a dangerous mission. They rode their horses almost due north across the plains to intersect the Marias River.

Why explore the Marias River any further? The captains hoped that the source of the river was high in Canada. If it was, the Marias would be a valuable water route to the rich Canadian fur trade.

The men found the Marias on July 22 and rode north along its banks for four days, alert for signs of Blackfeet all the time. By July 26, it was plain to Lewis that the Marias, dwindling rapidly, did not originate in Canada but somewhere much closer, on the plains. Disappointed, the men wheeled their horses around to return to the Missouri River.

Their relief at having escaped the notice of the Blackfeet was short-lived. On the afternoon of July 26, Lewis climbed a slight rise for a view of the country. He saw eight Blackfoot Indians with a herd of horses in the near distance. The Indians had spotted Drouillard, who was hunting and unaware that he was being watched. The explorers were outnumbered, but they could not flee and leave Drouillard. Putting on a bold face, Lewis advanced to meet the Blackfeet. He explained who they were and why they were there. He claimed that they were part of a large group and that the others were close at hand. The Indians assured Lewis that there were many more Blackfeet nearby.

That night the Indians and the explorers camped together in a large meadow. The Blackfeet seemed friendly, but Lewis's men took turns standing watch throughout the night. The Indians rose at dawn. Joseph Fields was on watch. He set his rifle down beside his brother Reuben's rifle for a moment. It was all the opportunity that the Indians needed.

One Indian grabbed both the Fields's rifles. Joseph bellowed at Reuben, who leaped up to help Joseph pursue the Indian. In the tussle that followed, Reuben stabbed the Indian to the heart. Drouillard wrestled with another Indian who had snatched his gun. A Blackfoot who had Lewis's rifle dropped it when Lewis threatened him with a pistol.

The horses had scattered. Drouillard and the Fields brothers ran after one herd. Lewis ran after a smaller herd that was also being pursued by two Indians. When the horses ran into a small rocky canyon, one of the Blackfeet turned and took aim at Lewis. The captain managed to shoot first and hit the Indian in the stomach. The Indian's bullet passed over Lewis's head so closely that it fanned his hair.

Lewis returned to find Drouillard and the Fields brothers. Two Indians were dead, and the others had withdrawn. If there were other Blackfeet nearby, they would soon be back in force. They chose the four best horses of those they had managed to gather and set the others free. They rode hard, stopping once to let the horses graze and again to eat a meal of buffalo. After dinner, they rode on over the plains in the moonlight. Were the Blackfeet following them?

Clark had had an easier time. He had gone south with the rest of the expedition and most of the horse herd. The Nez Perce knew of a pass across the Continental Divide that was much easier than the Lehmi Pass. They crossed the Divide by July 8 and soon reached the cache by the Jefferson River. Most of the men were overjoyed to see that the tobacco had survived well. The dugouts were in good condition, too.

The Gallatin River in the early morning fog

Some of the party went down the river in the dugouts, while others herded the horses along the shore. At Three Forks, Clark's group split. Sergeant Ordway and nine men took the dugouts down the Missouri to join Lewis's men at White Bear Island. They soon had the white pirogue back in the water. They floated down the Missouri, watching the banks for signs of Lewis and his group.

Clark's group, which included Charbonneau, Sacajawea, Pomp, and York, was now without boats of any type. They rode along the Gallatin River to the Yellowstone River with their herd of fifty horses. They were in Crow country. The Crow Indians were expert horse thieves. On July 21, the party awoke to find half the horses gone. No one had heard a thing.

Citadel Rock along the Missouri River in eastern Montana

Clark put four men in charge of the remaining horses. Everyone else boarded two small dugouts that the party had just built. They floated down the Yellowstone in dry, sunny weather. Clark went ashore to examine a huge, reddish, flat-topped butte. He named it Pompey's Tower in honor of little Pomp, to whom he had become very attached.

They drifted into the Missouri on August 3 without sighting a single Crow Indian. On August 8, Clark was astonished to see Sergeant Pryor and his men paddling frantically after them in round, wobbly, skin-covered bullboats. The stealthy Crows had spirited the rest of the herd away, and Pryor and his men had made some bullboats. They were glad to have caught up with Clark.

On August 11, two American trappers, Forest Hancock and Joseph Dickson, hailed the party. The explorers were amazed to see white men so far up the Missouri. The trappers reported that the Mandans, Hidatsas, and Arikaras were at war. The Teton Sioux were as aggressive as ever. The councils with the Indians seemed to have changed nothing.

Lewis and his men had seen no more signs of Blackfeet, but their worries were not over. They still had to find the rest of their party. They were several miles from the Missouri River when they heard rifle shots. They rode hard to reach the river and arrived to see the white pirogue rounding a bend. The men were firing their rifles as they traveled downstream.

Lewis's group was exhausted. They had ridden 120 miles (193 kilometers) in twenty-four hours. They turned their horses loose, threw the saddles in the river, and climbed aboard the pirogue. There was still a chance that the Blackfeet might attack them at the mouth of the Marias River, not far ahead. The red pirogue lay hidden there. They hurried to recover it and be on their way.

There was no sign of Blackfeet at the mouth of the Marias, but the red pirogue had rotted beyond hope of repair. They did not linger. On August 7, well out of Blackfoot territory, Lewis's group found a note from Clark near the mouth of the Yellowstone River. Clark had been there and had gone ahead.

On August 11, some men went ashore to hunt elk. Pierre Cruzatte was one of the hunters. The skilled riverboatman had poor eyesight. He shot at what he thought was a large elk. The "elk" turned out to be Lewis. Cruzatte's bullet passed through Lewis's buttocks. It was a painful but not fatal wound.

On August 12, they overtook Clark around noon. Clark was alarmed not to see Lewis among those in the pirogue. He hurried aboard and found Lewis stretched out on his stomach, feverish and in pain. Clark took over the task of cleaning and dressing his friend's wound.

The corps was happy to be reunited. The current carried them along at a swift pace, and they were soon at the Mandan Villages. Clark tried to persuade some chiefs to visit President Jefferson in Washington. Only Chief Sheheke agreed to go if his wife and child could accompany him. The French trader Rene Jessaume had persuaded Sheheke to make the trip, and Jessaume now insisted that he, his wife, and two children also be included. Clark grumbled, "We were obliged to agree."

There was a parting of ways at the Mandan Villages. Charbonneau was no longer needed to interpret; he was paid $500 for his services. Charbonneau, Sacajawea, and Pomp would stay in the villages.

The trappers Dickson and Hancock had returned to the Mandan Villages with the corps. They asked John Colter to return west with them to trap beaver. Lewis and Clark agreed to let Colter go only if no one else asked for a discharge before reaching St. Louis. Everyone agreed, and Colter was free to go. He left immediately with his trapper friends, paddling back in the direction from which he had just come.

The party left the Mandan Villages on August 17. Lewis's wound had healed well enough for him to walk, but he pushed himself so hard that the wound reopened. When the corps saw the Teton Sioux several days later, Clark had to handle things alone because Lewis was still not well.

Close to one hundred armed and mounted Sioux warriors lined the shores of the Missouri. They had nothing pleasant to say. Clark told them, "We viewed them as bad people . . . and to keep away from the river or we should kill every one of them." The conversation disintegrated into insults and threats. The corps kept to the middle of the river after this.

Farther downstream, the men visited Sergeant Floyd's gravesite. They began to meet traders who told them that, in the United States, they had been given up for dead.

The weather turned hot and sultry. The glare of sun on water gave the men sore eyes. Game became scarce. The great buffalo herds were now far behind them. Hungry though the men were, they were happy because home was near. Clark wrote, "The party appear perfectly contented and tell us they can live very well on pawpaws."

In September, they reached the small village of La Charette. The men cheered loudly at the sight of cows at pasture. Villagers poured out to greet them. It rained that evening, and the people of La Charette took the men into the shelter of their homes. Lewis and Clark spent the night in the tent of two Scotch traders, telling them about the West.

It was noon on September 23, 1806, when the jubilant explorers touched shore at St. Louis. A crowd gathered to see them disembark—a group of tanned, bearded, and roughly dressed men, back from the Western wilderness.

The captains did not spend that first night celebrating their return, as did the soldiers, but finishing reports and writing letters instead. The most important letter was addressed to President Jefferson.

Lewis began with the news of their safe arrival. They had discovered the most practical route across the country—a journey of 3,555 miles (5,721 kilometers) from the mouth of the Missouri to the point where the Columbia spills into the Pacific Ocean. The Missouri River portion of the trip "may be deemed safe and good; its difficulties arise from its falling banks, timber imbedded in bars and the steady rapidity of its current." The troublesome part was the trip from Great Falls to the Clearwater River. "Of this distance 200 miles is along a good road, and 140 miles over tremendous mountains for which 60 miles are covered with eternal snows." This leg of the journey could be accomplished only from the last part of June through September, on horseback. That left the traveler with 640 more miles (1,030 kilometers) of river travel to reach the Pacific Ocean.

Upper Multnomah Falls in the Columbia River Gorge. The last leg of their westward journey took Lewis and Clark through the stunning Columbia River Gorge.

Diary carried by William Clark on the expedition

Lewis knew that Jefferson would be disappointed. He had hoped for a far easier route, one suitable for trade with the Orient. However, they had found a natural resource that had a commercial value. Lewis wrote, "The Missouri and all its branches from the Cheyenne upwards abound more in beaver and common otter than any other streams on earth." The West was a fur trapper's paradise.

Lewis put in a word for Clark, with whom he shared equal credit for the success of the expedition. He added that he was anxious to find out if his mother was still alive. As a postscript, he added that everyone who had left the Mandan Villages with him was alive and in good health. Sergeant Floyd had been the expedition's only casualty.

Sergeant Ordway and some of the soldiers conducted Sheheke and Jessaume and their families to

Washington. They took with them crates full of plants, animals, and artifacts for the president. Clark and York went to Louisville to see Clark's family. From there Clark headed to Fincastle, Virginia, to visit Julia Hancock.

Lewis went home to Locust Hill. There he received a letter from President Jefferson: "I received, my dear Sir, with unspeakable joy your letter of September 23." Lewis arrived in Washington shortly after Christmas. Clark came to the capital in January. It had been difficult to leave Julia.

The captains were heroes. Dances, dinner parties, and receptions were given in their honor. Sheheke and his wife were honored as "The King and Queen of the Mandans."

Lewis sent Congress a list of the men who had served on the expedition. He praised George Drouillard, Joseph and Reuben Fields, John Shields, and Francois Labiche. He described Charbonneau as a "man of no peculiar merit." Lewis asked that the family of Charles Floyd receive some money.

Congress gave all the soldiers 320 acres (130 hectares) of land apiece and double pay, which amounted to between $10 and $16 per month. All were given an honorable discharge. Those who stayed in the army were offered choice posts.

The captains received 1,600 acres (648 hectares) of land apiece and double pay of $1,228 each. Lewis was appointed governor of the Louisiana Territory in March 1807. Clark was made the superintendent of Indian affairs for the territory and a brigadier general in the militia. He freed York and gave him a wagon and team of six horses. York established a freight-hauling business in Louisville, Kentucky.

Trappers like this one followed Lewis and Clark into the western wilderness.

The members of the western expedition went their separate ways. Four men returned to the West to trap beaver—John Colter, George Drouillard, John Potts, and Peter Wiser. John Potts and John Colter were canoeing near Three Forks in 1808 when a large group of Blackfoot warriors ordered them ashore. Potts panicked and shot an Indian. Potts was killed immediately, pierced with dozens of arrows.

Colter was given a slim chance to save himself. The Blackfeet took his weapons and clothing and told him to run for his life. They gave him a small head start, then pounded off after him. Colter had always been fast, but now he ran as he never had before. He outdistanced all but one of the warriors. When the Indian pulled even with him, Colter managed to kill the man with his own spear. Then he dove into a river and hid himself under some floating timber. The Blackfeet prowled the banks, but Colter escaped under cover of night. Naked and unarmed, he walked for a week until he reached a trader's fort.

Colter stayed in the West for several more years before returning to Missouri. He married and started a farm, but died in bed of "jaundice" in 1813 while he was still a young man.

George Drouillard, the resourceful hunter, scout, and interpreter, was ambushed by Blackfeet near Three Forks in 1810. He fought them as long as he could, using his horse for cover, but he was finally surrounded and shot in the back. Sergeant Gass lived to be the oldest member of the corps. He died at age ninety-nine in 1870. George Shannon became a judge and a district attorney in Missouri and dropped dead in court one day in 1836. Many of the men simply disappeared from the records of history.

Charbonneau, Sacajawea, and Pomp turned up unannounced in St. Louis in 1810 to visit Clark. Unable to adjust to life in the city, they returned to the West in 1811, leaving Pomp with Clark. Clark saw that Pomp received a good education. In 1816, twelve-year-old Pomp returned to life among the Indians. In 1824, he met Prince Maximillian, a German prince who was touring the American West. Maximillian took Pomp to Germany for five years, and when Pomp returned to the United States he became an army guide and mountain man. Pomp died in 1885, the last survivor of the western expedition.

With Clark's help, Charbonneau found a job as interpreter at a trader's fort. He was last seen in St. Louis in 1839, when he came to the city to collect some back pay owed him by a fur company. He went west again and was never heard of again.

There are several stories about Sacajawea. One story is that she died at age twenty-five of fever in a fort on the Missouri River. However, there is a great deal of evidence to support a far different version.

According to this version, the young Shoshoni woman who died was not Sacajawea but another of Charbonneau's many wives. Sacajawea left Charbonneau because he treated her badly. For a while she made her home among the Comanche Indians, marrying a warrior named Jerk Meat. After Jerk Meat died, she lived for a time among the Nez Perce. She ended her days among her own people, the Shoshoni, in the mountains of Wyoming. She died in her sleep at the age of ninety-four in April 1884.

The captains also went their separate ways to vastly different endings—Clark to a long and productive life and Lewis to an early and mysterious death.

Chapter 10
Different Paths

Lewis and Clark hoped to make money on a book of their adventures. Lewis found a publisher, an editor, and illustrators in Philadelphia. The projected book was not the first thing on Clark's mind, though. He was smitten with love for Julia Hancock. He visited her again on his way to St. Louis, and soon they were engaged to be married.

Lewis attended the wedding on January 5, 1808. Lewis himself wished to marry, too, or at least thought that he did. He was interested in several women, but his romances always seemed to be one-sided. He was not a ladies' man.

A full year after his appointment as governor of the Louisiana Territory, Lewis turned up in St. Louis to take his post. It was March 8, 1808. He had not been at all anxious to tackle this job. St. Louis was a wild town. Many worlds touched here: Indians, traders, trappers, and settlers all mingled together. The populace was British, French, Spanish, and American. There was a great deal of friction and violence.

Murders were commonplace in St. Louis. When an Indian was killed, the tribe was offered money to "cover" the death. As governor, Lewis announced that murders could no longer be "covered" with money. Murderers would be tried in courts of law. He insisted that settlers respect the Indians' rights and not intrude on their land. His efforts on the behalf of the Indians made him unpopular with many of the white settlers.

Lewis's secretary, Frederick Bates, was a petty and malicious man. He was jealous of Lewis and made trouble for him whenever he could. Lewis soon realized that he and Bates would never get along. He told Bates, "When we meet in public let us at least address each other with cordiality," but Bates would not do even that. Lewis soon began to drink too much.

The Mandan chief Sheheke, meanwhile, was still living among white society. Getting him home had proved to be a large problem, and it would be Lewis's undoing.

In 1807, Sergeant Pryor and some soldiers had escorted Sheheke and his family up the Missouri. All was well until they tried to pass the Arikara village. The Arikaras were angry because one of their chiefs had died in Washington. They attacked the party. Three soldiers were killed, and another died later of wounds. George Shannon was so badly hurt that his leg had to be amputated. The party returned to St. Louis with Sheheke.

The chief had been there ever since and had become quite a tiresome guest. The great attention that he had received in Washington convinced him of his own great importance. He described himself as the brother of the Great White Father in Washington. No longer would he deal with "little chiefs."

Sheheke became Lewis's problem. In 1809 Lewis signed a contract with the Missouri Fur Company, paying them $7,000 to get Sheheke home. The scheme worked. By autumn of 1809, Sheheke was home, where he told the Mandans of all the wondrous things he had seen. They thought he was a great liar. Sheheke soon wished he had remained among the white men.

Lewis had gotten rid of Sheheke, but now he was in deep trouble. The U.S. government refused to honor a voucher that Lewis had signed for $500 worth of trade goods for the Sheheke expedition. Had Jefferson been president, this would never have happened. But James Madison was president now. He had not appointed Lewis, and may have wanted someone else in Lewis's job. Or perhaps he did not understand the necessity of carrying gifts into Indian territory.

Lewis was devastated. Much more than $500 was at stake. Soon the word was out that the federal government refused to honor the debts that Lewis incurred as governor. Everyone to whom Lewis owed money flocked to his door, wanting immediate payment. In all, Lewis owed $4,000. He faced bankruptcy. Lewis prepared to go to Washington with his account books to argue his case. "All I wish is a full and fair investigation," he wrote.

In September 1809, Lewis and his servant Pernia boarded a Mississippi riverboat bound for New Orleans. Before they reached the city, Lewis was put off the boat at Chickasaw Bluffs (Memphis, Tennessee) because he had been acting strangely. Whether his behavior had been caused by heavy drinking, by malaria, or both, is not known. He recovered at Fort Pickering, cared for by a doctor who prescribed that he not drink any more alcohol.

James Madison

He now planned to travel overland to Washington. A Chickasaw Indian agent, Major James Neely, supplied horses and accompanied him. They took the Natchez Trace, a faint series of Indian trails that led through the dense forests of Tennessee.

A horse strayed one night, so Neely stayed behind in the morning to find it. Lewis, Pernia, and Neely's servant went on and stopped for the night at Grinders Stand, a settler's home.

The Grinders owned two small, rough cabins, and they sold meals and lodging to travelers. Only Mrs. Grinder was at home at the time. She gave Lewis the larger cabin for the night. He did not use the bed, but preferred to roll up in a buffalo skin on the floor. Mrs. Grinder slept in the other cabin, and the servants slept in the barn.

Two shots, perhaps three, broke the silence of the night. Lewis staggered from his cabin. He was horribly wounded in the head and the side. He begged Mrs. Grinder for water, but she refused to leave her cabin to help him.

Lewis lay alone in great pain until near dawn. That was when Pernia and Neely's servant found him lying in bed in his cabin. He begged them to shoot him, telling them, "I am no coward but I am so strong, so hard to die."

Lewis crawled out of the cabin and died outside at daybreak beside the trail. It was October 11, 1809, little more than three years after his triumphant return from the West. He was thirty-five years old.

Did Lewis kill himself, or was he murdered? No one knows for certain. He could have been shot by a robber. However, the evidence for suicide is stronger than the evidence for murder. Lewis had always suffered from deep depressions. He had been drinking heavily for several years, and he was facing financial ruin. At the time, his death was ruled a suicide.

He was buried where he fell. His good friend Clark read of Lewis's death in the newspapers on October 28. When Thomas Jefferson heard that Lewis was dead, he wrote a tribute: "Of courage undaunted, possessing a firmness and perseverance of purpose which nothing but impossibilities could divert from its direction, careful as a father of those committed to his charge. . . ."

Monument to Meriwether Lewis, erected over his grave 37 years after his death

Because Lewis's death was ruled a suicide, he was not honored in death as he deserved. Alexander Wilson, a naturalist and friend of Lewis, who visited his grave shortly after his death, wrote:

"He lies buried close by the common path with a few loose rails thrown over his grave. I gave Grinder money to put a post frame around it, to shelter it from the hogs and from the wolves, and he gave me his written promise."

Sadly, it was not until 1846 that a marker was placed over Lewis's grave.

Clark was the executor of Lewis's will. After all of his debts were settled, there was only $9.43 left, which went to Lewis's mother, Lucy Marks. Then there was the unfinished business of the book. Clark hired Nicholas Biddle to rewrite the journals in a more readable way. The account of the expedition was published in 1814, but it sold so poorly that the publisher went out of business.

As superintendent of Indian affairs, Clark negotiated at least thirty treaties with the Indians. He tried to be fair with them. They, in turn, liked him and called him the Red Hair Chief.

In 1813, President Madison appointed Clark territorial governor. He held the position until 1820, the year that the state of Missouri was created. He ran for governor of Missouri but was defeated, perhaps because white settlers viewed his stands as pro-Indian. Clark seemed not at all disappointed by his defeat and simply kept on working as superintendent of Indian affairs.

He and Julia, whom he still called Judy, had a large home on a farm set in rolling hills. Clark had built an Indian Hall, where he received his Indian guests. Not only Indians but also traders and trap-

William Clark in his later years

pers came to visit him, and he questioned them about the Western lands they had seen. He continued to work on his map, filling it in with the new information he received.

He and Julia were happily married. They had five children, but two of them—his only daughter, Mary, and his son Julius—died in childhood. Julia Clark died in 1820 after an illness. Clark remarried Julia's cousin, Harriet Kennerly Radford. She had been the other little girl whom he had met with Julia on that Virginia country road so many years earlier. Harriet and Clark had two children, one of whom died as an infant. Harriet died in 1831, and Clark did not marry again. He was a loving father and was always interested in the lives of his children. In addition to his own children, Clark acted as guardian for Sacajawea's and Charbonneau's son Pomp, for their daughter Lizette, and for Touissant, Charbonneau's son by another Indian woman.

William Clark died in St. Louis on September 1, 1838, in the house of his oldest son, Meriwether Lewis Clark. He was sixty-eight years old. Huge crowds attended the funeral of the Red Hair Chief.

By any measure, the Lewis and Clark expedition had been a great success. They penetrated a vast wilderness, carried out Jefferson's instructions fully, and returned with the loss of only one man. They brought back a wealth of information: maps, journals, plants, animals, rocks, Indian artifacts. Their observations on the Indian peoples—their customs, food, family life, clothing, religious beliefs, and vocabularies—were comprehensive. Theirs were the first written descriptions of the Nez Perce, Shoshoni, Flatheads, Yakimas, and others.

The expedition contributed much to knowledge of the natural sciences. The captains brought back several hundred plant and animal specimens and described hundreds more. Although the Indians had long been familiar with all of this wildlife, the captains' (predominantly Lewis's) descriptions were the first ever written about many plants and animals. Lewis, a careful observer, had missed very little.

One of Clark's major contributions was his map of the West. He had a remarkable eye for scale and distance. Given the instruments of the time, his map was very accurate. Together, the captains named riv-

One of Clark's maps, showing the various tribes of Indians living around the Columbia River

ers, meadows, passes, and rock formations. Though some of the names have changed, many are the same.

Lewis and Clark opened the West to Americans' imagination. Before the expedition, it was thought that the West contained such wonders as a mountain of salt or a tribe of white Indians descended from Welshmen. Lewis and Clark returned with an account of the real wonders of the West: endless herds of buffalo, bubbling hot streams, whitewater rivers, fierce grizzly bears, and massive, snow-covered mountains. Americans were no longer content to simply daydream about the rich opportunities of the West.

Ferns along Still Creek in Mount Hood National Forest, Oregon

Oregon's Mount Jefferson. In the early decades of the 1800s, fur trappers and mountain men plied the Western wilderness in search of beavers and other fur-bearers.

Mountain men arrived first to trap beaver in the streams and rivers. The fur-trade era lasted only as long as did the popularity of beaver-fur hats in Europe. When silk hats became the fashion, the fur era ended. Next came the settlers, families in covered Conestoga wagons. American claims to the Pacific Northwest were immeasurably strengthened by Lewis's and Clark's exploration. That region became part of the United States. In time, there were ten states along the Lewis and Clark trail: Missouri, Kansas, Iowa, Nebraska, North Dakota, South Dakota, Montana, Idaho, Washington, and Oregon.

The western expansion had its price. For all that the United States and its farmers and ranchers gained, much was lost. Indians were decimated by sickness, driven from their land, and herded onto reservations.

*Ramona Falls in Mount Hood
Wilderness, Oregon*

Many of the West's rich resources were squandered.
The buffalo were slaughtered almost to the point of
extinction.

Some species that the captains had admired, such
as Audubon's mountain sheep, became extinct.
Ranchers and farmers shot, trapped, and poisoned
wolves and cougars. Most of the wolves remaining on
the North American continent are now found in
Canada and Alaska. Cougars are scarce. Even the
rivers have changed. Dammed and diverted, the
Missouri and the Columbia are no longer the wild
rivers that Lewis and Clark rode.

A modern-day traveler, following the Lewis and
Clark trail, could not see all that they saw but would
have to imagine it—the Western land, still wild, fresh,
and untouched.

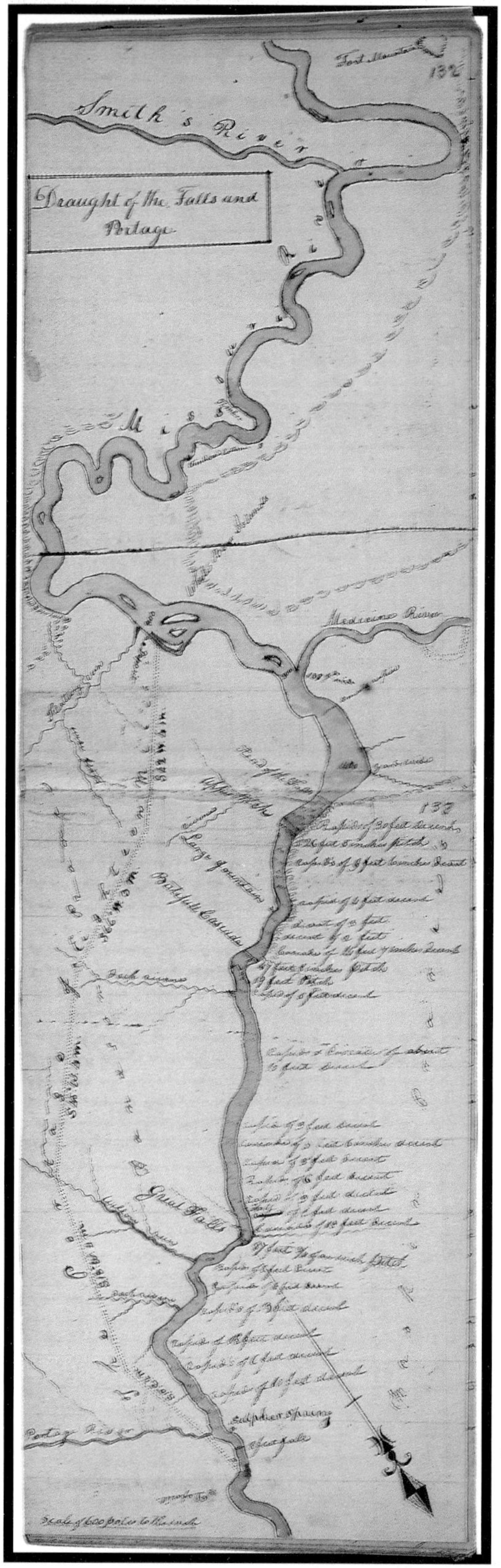

Fort Mau...

Smith's River

Draught of the Falls and
Portage

Medicine River

132

Great Falls

Portage River

Sulphur Spring

Scale of 600 poles to the inch

Appendix

Here are just a few of the items from Meriwether Lewis's long list of supplies purchased for the expedition:

Indian Presents

1 Piece Red Flannel 47 1/2 yds.
1 doz. Ivory Combs
4 doz. Butcher Knives
12 doz. Pocket Looking Glasses
2 doz. Nonesopretty
73 Bunches Beads
2 doz. Earrings
500 Brooches
72 Rings
2800 Fish Hooks
4600 Needles
3 gross Curtain Rings

Camp Equipage

4 Tin Horns
3 doz. Pint Tumblers
8 Pieces Cat Gut for Mosquito Curtain
6 Brass Kettles
2 doz. Table Spoons
2 Hand Saws
9 Chisels
12 lbs. Castile Soap
6 Brass Inkstands
100 Quills

Provisions

193 lbs. P. Soup
45 Flannel Shirts
15 Pairs Blue Wool Overalls
36 Pairs Stockings
20 Frocks
30 Pairs Shirts
20 Pairs Shoes

Timeline of Events in Lewis's and Clark's Lifetimes

1770—William Clark is born in Albemarle County, Virginia

1774—Meriwether Lewis is born in Albemarle County, Virginia

1789—Clark joins the Kentucky militia

1794—Lewis joins the Virginia militia

1801—Lewis is appointed President Jefferson's secretary

1803—The United States purchases the Louisiana Territory from France; Lewis and Clark are appointed to lead a western expedition

1804—**May 14**. The expedition leaves from Camp Wood, Missouri
August 2. In present-day Nebraska, they meet Oto Indians
August 20. Sergeant Charles Floyd dies near Sioux City, Iowa
October 25. They reach the Mandan Villages in North Dakota, build Fort Mandan, and camp for the winter; Charbonneau and Sacajawea join the expedition

1805—**April 7**. They leave Fort Mandan and continue west
June 13. Lewis arrives at the Great Falls of the Missouri
July 25. They discover the Three Forks of the Missouri
September 11-22. They cross the Continental Divide
November 14-18. In separate parties, Lewis and Clark reach the Pacific Ocean; they build Fort Clatsop and camp for the winter

1806—**March 23**. The expedition heads home
September 23. The explorers arrive back in St. Louis

1807—Lewis is appointed governor and Clark is made superintendent of Indian affairs for Louisiana Territory

1808—Clark marries Julia Hancock

1809—**October 11**. Meriwether Lewis dies at Grinders Stand in Tennessee

1813—Clark becomes territorial governor

1820—Clark returns to his Indian affairs post; Julia dies

1831—Clark's second wife, Harriet, dies

1838—**September 1**. William Clark dies in St. Louis

Glossary of Terms

cache—A place where things are hidden or stored

capsize—To overturn

carcass—A dead body

cavort—To prance around

celestial navigation—A method of steering by the stars

corps—A group of people involved in a joint activity

dugout—A boat made by hollowing out a log

eclipse—The darkening of the sun or moon when the earth's shadow covers it

floe—A floating sheet of ice

fluent—Able to speak a language smoothly

fossil—A plant or animal preserved in stone

garrison—A military post

gauntlet—A double line of men who strike a wrongdoer

keelboat—A shallow riverboat for hauling goods

militia—A local, rather than national, army

naturalist—Someone who studies plants and animals

nurseryman—A person who cultivates plants

pemmican—A mixture of dried, pounded meat and melted fat

pirogue—A boat similar to a canoe

portage—To carry boats and supplies on land

poultice—A warm, medicated cloth applied to a sore body part

quadrupeds—Four-legged animals

ravine—A narrow valley with steep sides

rheumatism—Inflamed and painful muscles or joints

talons—Claws

voyageurs—French boatmen skilled in wilderness travel

Bibliography

For further reading, see:

Brown, Marion Marsh. *Sacagawea: Indian Interpreter to Lewis and Clark*. Chicago: Childrens Press, 1988.

Cutright, Paul R. *Lewis and Clark: Pioneering Naturalists*. Urbana: University of Illinois Press, 1969.

DeVoto, Bernard, editor. *The Journals of Lewis and Clark*. Boston: Houghton Mifflin Co., 1953.

Eide, Ingvard Henry, compiler. *American Odyssey: The Journey of Lewis and Clark*. NY: Rand, McNally and Co., 1969.

Hawke, David Freeman. *Those Tremendous Mountains: The Story of the Lewis and Clark Expedition*. NY: Norton, 1985.

Jackson, Donald, editor. *Letters of the Lewis and Clark Expedition with Related Documents*. 2 volumes. Urbana: University of Illinois Press, 1978.

Lavender, David. *The Way to the Western Sea*. NY: Harper & Row, 1988.

——. *Westward Vision*. NY: McGraw-Hill, 1956.

Moulton, Gary E., editor. *Atlas of the Lewis and Clark Expedition*. Lincoln: University of Nebraska Press, 1983.

Petersen, David and Coburn, Mark. *Meriwether Lewis and William Clark: Soldiers, Explorers, and Partners in History*. Chicago: Childrens Press, 1988.

Salisbury, Albert and Jane. *Two Captains West*. NY: Bramhall House, 1968.

Stein, R. Conrad. *The Story of the Lewis and Clark Expedition*. Chicago: Childrens Press, 1978.

Thwaites, Reuben G., editor. *Original Journals of the Lewis and Clark Expedition*. 8 volumes. Reprint of 1904 edition. Salem, NH: Arno, 1972.

Index

Page numbers in boldface type indicate illustrations.

Albemarle County, Virginia, 15, 19

American War of Independence, 15, 19

animals, **22-23,** 40, **40, 41,** 52, 55, **56,** 58, **61, 85, 86-87,** 104, 115-119. *See also* names of specific animals

antelope, pronghorn, 40-41, **41,** 50

Appaloosas (horses), 92

Arikara Indians, 44, 49, 100, 110

Bates, Frederick, 110

Bear's Tooth Mountain, **32**

Beaverhead River, 68, 74

Biddle, Nicholas, 113

birthplace: Clark's, 8; Lewis's, 8, 15

Bitterroot Mountains, 75

Bitterroot River, 76, **76**

Black Cat (Mandan chief), 47, 50

Blackfoot Indians, 70, 95-97, 100, 106

Blue Ridge Mountains, 15

Bonaparte, Napoleon, 28, **28**

British fur trade, 38-39

buffalo, 39, 40, **40,** 50, 51, 60-61, 74, 75, **75,** 76, 102, 119

bullboats, 49, **49,** 99

Cameahwait (Shoshoni chief), 70-71, 74

Camp Wood, Missouri, 8, 30-33

canoes, 7, 12, **57,** 85, 90

Cascade Mountains, 81

Celilo Falls, 80, 88

Charbonneau, Jean Baptiste ("Pomp"), 51, 53, 57, 62, 64, 84, 98, 99, 101, 106, 115

Charbonneau, Lizette, 115

Charbonneau, Touissant (senior), 10, 49, 53, 55, 57, 64, 84, 98, 101, 105, 106, 115

Charbonneau, Touissant (junior), 115

Chinook Indians, 10, 82-83, **82,** 87-88

Citadel Rock, **99**

Clark, Ann (mother), 19

Clark, George Rogers (brother), 19, **19,** 20

Clark, Harriet Kennerly Radford (second wife), 21,115

Clark, John (father), 19, 20

Clark, Julia Hancock (first wife), 21, 58, 105, 107, 114-115

Clark, Meriwether Lewis (son), 115

Clark, William, pictures of, **2, 5, 37, 48, 66, 67, 68, 79, 82, 114**

Clarksville, Indiana, 20, 30

Clatsop Indians, 10, 82

Clearwater River, 78-79, 89, 92, 103

Colter, John, 31, 101, 106

Columbia River, 7, 12-13, 66-67, 78-81, **79, 80,** 83-84, **81, 83,** 87, 89, **89,** 103, **116,** 119

Columbia River Gorge, **27, 103**

Columbian Plain, 78-79

Comanche Indians, 107

Continental Divide, 66, 74, 76, 95, 97

cottonwood trees, 53, **53,** 63

cougars, 61, **61,** 119

coyotes, 40

Crow Indians, 70, 98-99

Cruzatte, Pierre, 31, 35, 36, 43, 57, 100, 102

death: Clark's, 115; Lewis's, 112-113

deer, 40

Deschamps, Baptiste, 33

Detroit, Michigan, 18

Dickson, Joseph, 100, 101

drinking problem, Lewis's, 110, 111, 112

Drouillard, George, 31, 36, 44, 51, 57, 64, 71, 78, 85, 93, 95-97, 105, 106

dugouts, 7, 12, 53, 65, 80, 85, 88

education: Clark's, 9, 19; Lewis's, 9, 16

elk, 84, 100

expedition: invitation to lead, 8-9, 21; preparations for, 23-33

Experiment (boat), 65

Fallen Timbers, Battle of, 20

Fields, Reuben and Joseph, 31, 93, 95-97, 105

fish and fishing, 10-11, **62, 72-73,** 79, **80,** 82

Flathead Indians, 76, 115

Floyd, Charles, 32, 39, 102, 104, 105

food, 10-11, 24, 36, 43, 44, 50, 51, 64, 77-80, 82, 83, 84, 91, 102

Fort Clatsop, 84-85, **84**

Fort Greenville, Ohio, 8, 18, 20

Fort Mandan, 48-50, **49,** 52, 64, 85

Fort Pickering, 111

fossil, 41

fur-trade era, 118

fur trappers, **106**

Gallatin River, 67, 98, **98**

Gass, Patrick, 31, 39, 106; drawings by, **37, 57**

Gates of the Mountains, **65**

geography skills, 9-10, 52

Georgia, 16

Gibson, George, 31

Gilmer, Peachy, 16

Goodrich, Silas, 31

governor of Louisiana Territory, Clark as, 114

governor of Louisiana Territory, Lewis as, 105, 109-111

Gray's Bay, 13, 83

Great Falls of the Missouri, 59-60, **60,** 64, 76, 95, 103, **120**

Grinders Stand, 112

grizzly bears, 56, **56,** 60-61

guns, 24, 70, 73, 91, 93

Hancock, Forest, 100, 101

Hancock, Julia. See Clark, Julia Hancock

Harpers Ferry, 24

Hidatsa Indians, 100

homes: Clark's, 19; Lewis's, 15, 16

horses, 48, 67, 70, 73, 74, 88, 91-92, **92**

illnesses, 39, 47, 62-63, 88

Indians, 9, 10-11, 12, 15, 19, 20, 24, 28, 31, **37,** 40, **43,** 52, 56, 59, **68, 75, 80, 90, 92,** 109-110, 113, 115, 117. *See also under* Arikara, Blackfoot, Chinook, Clatsop, Comanche, Crow, Hidatsa, Mandan, Minitari, Nez Perce, Oto, Shoshoni, Sioux, Sokulk, Tillamook, Walla Walla, and Yakima Indians

Iowa, 36

jackrabbits, 40

James River, 38-39

Jefferson, Thomas, 8, **8,** 9, 15, 18, 20, 23, 26, 28-29, 52, 66, 101, 103-105, 111, 114

Jefferson River, 67-68, 74, 97

Jerk Meat (Comanche warrior), 107

Jessaume, Rene, 49, 101, 104

journals of the expedition, 36, 38, 52, **62, 81, 83,** 85, **89, 104,** 109, 113, 115-116, **116, 120**

Judith River, **54-55**, 58, **58**
Kaskaskia, Illinois, 30
keelboat, 25, **25**, 33, 36, 52
Kennerly, Harriet. *See* Clark,
    Harriet Kennerly Radford
La Charette (village), 102
La Liberte, 36, 39
Labiche, Francois, 35, 102, 105
Lehmi Pass, 74, 97
LePage, Baptiste, 49, 55
letter of acceptance, Clark's, **21**
Lewis, Jane (sister), 16
Lewis, John (father), 15
Lewis (Marks), Lucy (mother),
    15, 16, 113
Lewis, Meriwether, pictures of,
    **2, 5, 9, 37, 48, 66, 67, 68, 79,
    82**
Lewis, monument to, **113**
Lewis, Reuben (brother), 16
Lewis and Clark Pass, 95
Lewis and Clark State Park,
    Iowa, **25**
Lewis Rock, **69**
Lewiston, Idaho, **4**
Locust Hill (Lewis home), 15, 16
Lolo Trail, 76-78, 92-93
Lost Trail, 75, 76
Louisiana Purchase, **29**
Louisiana Territory, 28-29, 105
Louisville, Kentucky, 19, 20,
    105
Mackenzie, Alexander, 8
Madison, James, 111, **111**, 114
Madison River, 67
Mandan Indians, **5**, 45, **46-47**,
    47-50, **48**, 100, 110
Mandan Villages, 33, 44-45, **45**,
    47-48, **48**, 55, 101, 104
maps and mapmaking, 10, 20,
    28, **29, 33**, 36, 52, **81, 83**, 85,
    89, 114, 115-116, **116, 120**
Marias River, 59, **59**, 64, 93, 95-
    96, 100
Marks, John (Lewis's step-
    father), 16
Marks, John Hastings (Lewis's
    half-brother), 16
Marks, Lucy. *See* Lewis
    (Marks), Lucy
Marks, Mary (Lewis's half-
    sister), 16
marriage, Clark's, 109
Maximillian (German prince),
    107
Memphis, Tennessee, 18, 20,
    111
military service: Clark's, 19-20;
    Lewis's, 18
Minitari Indians, 47, 48, 49, 52,
    70

Mississippi River, 8, 9, 20, 26,
    28, 30
Missouri, 36, 114
Missouri Breaks, 58
Missouri Fur Company, 111
Missouri River, 8, 26-27, 30,
    32, 34-35, 35, 42, **45, 54-55,**
    59, **60, 65,** 66-67, 85, 93, 96,
    99, 103-104, 110, 119, **120**
Monroe, James, 28
Montana, **54-55,** 56, **58, 59, 76,
    99**
Monticello (Jefferson's home),
    15, 52, **52**
Mount Hood National Forest,
    Oregon, **86-87, 90, 117**
Mount Jefferson, Oregon, **118**
Mulberry Hill (Clark home), 19
Natchez Trace, 112
nature, observations of and
    specimens from, 9, 24-25, 36,
    52, 85, 104-105, 115-116
Nebraska, 36
Neely, James, 112
New Orleans, Louisiana, 28,
    52, 111
Nez Perce Indians, 73, 78-79,
    91-93, 95, 97, 107, 115
North Dakota, 33, 44, **71**
Northwest Passage, 8, 13, 27,
    103-104
Ohio River, 20, 26, **26,** 30
Old Toby (guide), 74-78
Ordway, John, 32, 38, 98, 104
Oto Indians, 36-38
Pacific Northwest, 7-8, 10-13,
    27, 118
Pacific Ocean, **6-7,** 8, 12, 13, **13,**
    81, 83-84, **84,** 103
Peale's Natural History
    Museum, 52
Pernia (Lewis's servant), 111,
    112
personalities: Clark's, 9;
    Lewis's, 9, 16, 32
petroglyphs, **4**
pirogues, 30, 33, 39, 53, 56-57,
    64, 100
Platte River, 35
Pomp. *See* Charbonneau, Jean
    Baptiste
Pompey's Tower, 99
Portage Creek, 62, 64, 95
portaging, 27, 63-64, **63,** 88,
    120
Potts, John, 106
prairie dogs, 40, 41, **41**
Pryor, Nathaniel, 32, 99, 110
Red Hair Chief (Clark's
    nickname), 113, 115
Reed, Moses, 39

Rocky Mountains, 28-29, 52, 64,
    66-67, **66,** 74-78, 81
Sacajawea, 10, 49, 51, 53, 57,
    62-63, 64, 67, **67,** 71, **71,** 82-
    83, **82,** 84, 98, 101, 106, 115
Saint Charles, Missouri, 33, 35
Saint Louis, Missouri, 8, 30-31,
    33, 102, 106, 109-110
salmon, 10-11, **72-73,** 79-80, **80,**
    82, 88-89
Salmon River, 74, 75
Seaman (Lewis's dog), 10, 30,
    53, 58, 87
Shannon, George, 31, 93, 106,
    110
Sheheke (Mandan chief), 47, 50,
    101, 104, 105, 110-111
Shields, John, 31, 36, 44, 50, 69,
    105
Shoshoni Indians, 49, 62, 67-71,
    73-75, 77, 115
Sioux Indians, 38-40, 41-44, **42,**
    48, 51, 53, 100, 101-102
Snake River, 79, 89
Sokulk Indians, 10
South Dakota, **34-35,** 40
Spaniards, 20, 28
superintendent of Indian
    affairs, Clark as, 105, 113-
    114
Three Forks, 67, **67, 69,** 98, 106
Tillamook Indians, 10, 84
trading with Indians, 10-12, 24,
    37, 38-39, 40, 88-89
Traveller's Rest (valley), 76, 93
Virginia, 8, **14-15,** 15, 16, 17, **17,**
    19, 21
Walla Walla Indians, 89-90
Warfington, Corporal Richard,
    33, 52
Warner, William, 31
Washington, D. C., 52, 101, 104,
    105, 112
Washington, George, 18, **18,** 20
Washington (State), 7
Wayne, "Mad" Anthony, 20, **20**
Whiskey Rebellion, 18
White Bear Island, 64, 95, 98
Wieppe Plain, 92-93
Wilson, Alexander, 113
Wiser, Peter, 106
wolves, 50, 119
Wyoming, 107
Yakima Indians, 79-80, 89-90,
    115
Yellept (Walla Walla chief), 89-
    90
Yellowstone River, 56, 93, **94-
    95,** 98-99, 100
York (Clark's slave), 10, **10, 11,**
    20, 44, 64, 67, 70, 71, 98, 105

Picture Identifications for Chapter Opening Spreads

6-7—Pacific Ocean along Oregon's southern coast

14-15—Scenic Virginia, home of Jefferson, Lewis, and Clark

22-23—Fawn in the forest

34-35—The Missouri River south of Pierre, South Dakota

46-47—Painting of a Mandan dance, by George Catlin

54-55—Area in Montana where the Judith and Missouri rivers meet

72-73—Salmon running upstream

86-87—Bear grass and rhododendron, Mount Hood National Forest, Oregon

94-95—Sunset on the Yellowstone River in Wyoming

108-109—A moss-carpeted forest floor

Acknowledgment

For a critical reading of the manuscript, our thanks to John Parker, Ph.D., Curator, James Ford Bell Library, University of Minnesota, Minneapolis, Minnesota

Picture Acknowledgments

© American Philosophical Society Library, Philadelphia—81, 83, 89, 116, 120

The Bettmann Archive—5, 92

© Reinhard Brucker—25, 34-35, 49 (2 pictures)

Steven Gaston Dobson—Cover, 10

© Virginia R. Grimes—69, 113

© Jerry Hennen—99

Historical Pictures Service, Chicago—19, 20, 28, 33, 45, 66, 114

Library of Congress—37, 79

Montana Historical Society—11

North Wind Picture Archives—2 (2 pictures), 9, 17, 21, 26, 29, 32, 38, 42, 43, 52, 57, 60, 62, 63, 65, 68, 75, 77, 80, 85, 104, 106

© Rob Outlaw—54-55, 58, 59, 98

© Photri—46-47, 48 (bottom), 67, 82

R/C Photo Agency: © Richard L. Capps—71

Chris Roberts Represents: © Slocomb—76

H. Armstrong Roberts: © Camerique—14-15; © D. Muench—108-109

© Bob and Ira Spring—4, 70, 84 (bottom)

Tom Stack & Associates: © Hal Clason—94-95

State Historical Society, North Dakota Heritage Center, Bismarck—48 (top)

SuperStock—22-23

© Steve Terrill—6-7, 13, 27, 84 (top), 86-87, 90, 103, 117, 118, 119

U.S. Bureau of Printing and Engraving—8, 18, 111

Valan: © Wayne Lankinen—40; © Wilf Schurig—41 (top); © D. W. Schmidt—41 (bottom); © J. R. Page—53; © Johnny Johnson—56; © Halle Flygare Photos Ltd.—61; © Aubrey Lang—72-73

About the Author

Christine Fitz-Gerald holds a B.A. in English Literature from Ohio University and a Masters in Management from Northwestern University. She has been employed by the Quaker Oats Company and by General Mills. Most recently, she was a strategic planner for a division of Honeywell, Inc. in Minneapolis. She now resides in Chicago with her husband and three young children. Her Childrens Press titles include *I Can Be a Reporter* and, in the *Encyclopedia of Presidents* series, *James Monroe* and *William Henry Harrison.*